STUDIA POHL: SERIES MAIOR

DISSERTATIONES SCIENTIFICAE DE REBUS ORIENTIS ANTIQUI

18

E PONTIFICIO INSTITUTO BIBLICO
ROMAE

KONRAD VOLK

with the collaboration of

Silvano Votto and Annette Zgoll

A SUMERIAN READER

Second, revised edition

EDITRICE PONTIFICIO ISTITUTO BIBLICO
ROMA 1999

The Pontifical Biblical Institute dedicates this series to the memory of P. Alfred Pohl, founder of its Faculty of Ancient Near Eastern Studies. *Studia Pohl* reproduces in offset studies on Ancient Near Eastern history and philology, and is intended particularly to benefit younger scholars who wish to present the results of their doctoral studies to a wider public.

ISBN 88-7653-610-8

Piazza della Pilotta 35 – 00187 Roma, Italia

To the memory of

Johannes Jacobus Adrianus van Dijk

(28.1.1915 - 14.5.1996)

and

Hermann Behrens SCJ

(15.7.1944 - 2.8.1996)

CONTENTS

PREFACE

This SUMERIAN READER contains 44 texts of varying contents: royal inscriptions, legal, and economic documents. For pedagogical reasons literary texts are not included. Some of the texts are accompanied by a transliteration and/or version in Neo-Assyrian so that the student can learn the Neo-Assyrian forms which are of basic importance for the use of the sign list in this book and, in general, for most assyriological sign lists.

Each inscription is to be studied with the help of the sign list, the list of phonetic values, and the glossaries. In this SUMERIAN READER I have intentionally not dealt with questions of grammar. Instead, the reader is referred to two rather recent publications on the subject: *M.-L. Thomsen, The Sumerian Language. An Introduction to its History and Grammatical Structure. Mesopotamia 10. Copenhagen Studies in Assyriology (Copenhagen 1984)*, and *P. Attinger, Éléments de linguistique sumérienne. La construction de* du_{11}*/e/di «dire» (Orbis Biblicus et Orientalis, Sonderband; Fribourg/Göttingen 1993)*. For a general introduction to Sumerology, *W.H.Ph. Römer, Die Sumerologie. Versuch einer Einführung in den Forschungsstand nebst einer Bibliographie in Auswahl. (Nimwegener sumerologische Studien 2. Alter Orient und Altes Testament, 238. Kevelaer/Neukirchen-Vluyn 1994)* is highly recommended.

This book began as a manuscript called *"Sumerische Chrestomathie. Texte zusammengestellt, teilweise transkribiert, in neuassyrische Zeichenformen übertragen und mit Glossar und Zeichenliste versehen" (Eschbach 1978)* that I wrote when I was a young student of Assyriology at Freiburg i. Br. It soon proved to be a very useful and requested tool for many beginning students of Sumerian. Over the years a good number of both teachers and students who used my *"Sumerische Chrestomathie"* gave me their personal notes, corrections and improvements, for which I am very grateful. I want to thank the following persons for such help: J. Keetman, B. Kienast, G.J. Selz and H. Steible, Freiburg; H. Behrens, Philadelphia; J. van Dijk, Rome/Amsterdam; D.O. Edzard and M.P. Streck, Munich; C. Wilcke, Leipzig; P. Attinger, Bern; M.J. Geller, London; W.G. Lambert, Birmingham; W.R. Mayer, Rome.

When I was already about to forget my first 'printed' effort in Assyriology that I issued privately as the demand arose, Fr. W.R. Mayer SJ of the Pontifical Biblical Institute in Rome suggested that I produce an English version of this book and publish it as a volume in the Pontifical Biblical Institute's Series Studia Pohl. Then my friend and colleague from my Roman days, Fr. Silvano Votto SJ, not only translated the whole manuscript into English but also made a considerable number of improvements. To him I owe very special thanks for his invaluable contributions to this book, now called A SUMERIAN READER. During the final stage of preparing this SUMERIAN READER, Annette Zgoll [Ganter] (Munich) was kind enough to type most of the glossaries on the computer and also to make a number of useful suggestions.

St. Peter 1997 / Tübingen 1999 — Konrad Volk

BIBLIOGRAPHIC ABBREVIATIONS

With some exceptions and additions, bibliographic abbreviations follow the standard abbreviations in the *Assyrian Dictionary of the Oriental Institute of the University of Chicago* (Chicago/Glückstadt, 1956ff.), W. von Soden, *Akkadisches Handwörterbuch* (Wiesbaden 1958-81), and *The Sumerian Dictionary of the University Museum of the University of Pennsylvania*, edited by Å.W. Sjöberg (Philadelphia 1984ff.).

ABZ	R. Borger, Assyrisch-babylonische Zeichenliste (Kevelaer/Neukirchen-Vluyn 1978 [AOAT 33]; Ergänzungsband [AOAT 33A]; 1981)
AcOr	Acta Orientalia (Copenhagen 1922ff.)
AEM I/1	J.-M. Durand, Archives épistolaires de Mari I/1 (Paris 1988)
AfO	Archiv für Orientforschung, vols. 3ff. [vols. 1-2 = AfK] (Berlin, Graz and Horn 1926ff.)
AnOr	Analecta Orientalia (Rome 1931ff.)
AOAT	Alter Orient und Altes Testament. Veröffentlichungen zur Kultur und Geschichte des Alten Orients und des Alten Testaments (Kevelaer/Neukirchen-Vluyn 1969ff.)
AoF	Altorientalische Forschungen (Berlin 1974ff.)
AoN	J. Bauer, Altorientalistische Notizen (Würzburg 1976ff.)
AS	Assyriological Studies (Chicago 1931ff.)
ASJ	Acta Sumerologica Japonica (Hiroshima 1979ff.)
AulOr	Aula Orientalis (Sabadell [Barcelona] 1983ff.)
AWL	J. Bauer, Altsumerische Wirtschaftstexte aus Lagaš (Rome 1972)
BaF	Baghdader Forschungen (Mainz 1979ff.)
BaM	Baghdader Mitteilungen (Berlin 1960ff.)
BCSMS	Bulletin of the Canadian Society for Mesopotamian Studies (Toronto 1981ff.)
BFE	M. Krebernik, Die Beschwörungen aus Fara und Ebla. Untersuchungen zur ältesten keilschriftlichen Beschwörungsliteratur (Hildesheim / Zürich / New York 1984)
BiOr	Bibliotheca Orientalis (Leiden 1943ff.)
BSA	Bulletin on Sumerian Agriculture (Cambridge [U.K.] 1984ff.)
CAD	The Assyrian Dictionary of the Oriental Institute of the University of Chicago (Chicago/Glückstadt, 1956ff.)
CIRPL	E. Sollberger, Corpus des inscriptions 'royales' présargoniques de Lagaš (Genève 1956)

clergé	D. Charpin, Le clergé d'Ur au siècle d'Hammurabi (XIXe-XVIIIe siècles av. J.-C.) (Genève / Paris 1986)
CM	Cuneiform Monographs (Groningen 1992ff.)
CRRA	Compte rendu de la ... Rencontre Assyriologique Internationale. 19: P. Garelli (ed.), Le palais et la royauté (Archéologie et Civilisation; Paris 1974)
CT	Cuneiform Texts from Babylonian Tablets in the British Museum (London 1896ff.)
Cultic Calendars	M.E. Cohen, The Cultic Calendars of the Ancient Near East (Bethesda [MD] 1993)
DC	Découvertes en Chaldée par E. de Sarzec, ouvrage accompagné de planches, publié par les soins de L. Heuzey, avec le concours de A. Amiaud et F. Thureau-Dangin pour la partie épigraphique. Premier volume: texte (Paris 1884-1912). Second volume: Partie épigraphique et planches (Paris 1884-1912)
DV 3/II	M.V. Nikolskij, Dokumenty chozjajstvennoj otčetnosti drevnejšej epochi Chaldei iz sobranija N.P. Lichačeva. Drevnosti Vostočnyja Trudy Vostočnoj Komissii Imperatorskago Moskovskago Archeologičeskago Obščestva 3/II (St. Petersburg 1908)
ÉLS	P. Attinger, Éléments de linguistique sumérienne. La construction de du_{11}/e/di «dire» (Fribourg / Göttingen 1993)
Épithètes royales	M.-J. Seux, Épithètes royales akkadiennes et sumériennes (Paris 1967)
Familiengründung	C. Wilcke, Familiengründung im Alten Babylonien. In: Geschlechtsreife und Legitimation zur Zeugung (= Kindheit Jugend Familie I, E.W. Müller, ed.). Veröffentlichungen des Instituts für Historische Anthropologie 3 (Freiburg / München 1985) 213-317
FAOS	Freiburger altorientalische Studien (Wiesbaden, Stuttgart 1975ff.)
FI	M. Civil, The Farmer's Instructions. A Sumerian Agricultural Manual. Aula Orientalis - Supplementa 5 (Sabadell [Barcelona] 1994)
Fö	W. Förtsch, Altbabylonische Wirtschaftstexte aus der Zeit Lugalanda's und Urukagina's (VS 14/1, Leipzig 1916)
Fossey	Ch. Fossey, Manuel d'Assyriologie, Tome II. Évolution des cunéiformes (Paris 1926)
FT	H. de Genouillac, Fouilles de Tello (Paris 1934-1936)
Gazetteer	A.R. George, House Most High. The Temples of Ancient Mesopotamia. Mesopotamian Civilizations 5 (Winona Lake 1993) 63-161: *'Gazetteer of Ceremonial Names'*.

HANE/S	History of the Ancient Near East / Studies (Padova 1990ff.)
HSAO	Heidelberger Studien zum Alten Orient - A. Falkenstein zum 17. September 1966 (Wiesbaden 1967)
HUCA	Hebrew Union College Annual (Cincinnati 1924ff.)
Iraq	Iraq. Published by the British School of Archaeology in Iraq (London 1934ff.)
Ist.Mitt.	Istanbuler Mitteilungen. Herausgegeben vom Deutschen Archäologischen Institut, Abteilung Istanbul (Istanbul and Tübingen 1933ff.)
ITT	Inventaire des tablettes de Tello conservées au Musée Impérial Ottoman (Paris 1910-1921)
JAOS	Journal of the American Oriental Society (New Haven 1893ff.)
JCS	Journal of Cuneiform Studies (New Haven, Cambridge [Mass.], Philadelphia, Baltimore 1947ff.)
JNES	Journal of Near Eastern Studies (Chicago 1942ff.)
JQR (NS)	Jewish Quarterly Review (Philadelphia 1910/11ff.)
Kutscher Memorial Vol.	*kinattūtu ša dārâti.* Raphael Kutscher Memorial Volume. Edited by A.F. Rainey, A. Kempinski, M. Sigrist and D. Ussishkin (Tel Aviv 1993).
Labat	R. Labat, Manuel d'épigraphie akkadienne (Paris 1976^{5})
LAK	A. Deimel, Liste der archaischen Keilschriftzeichen von Fara (WVDOG 40, Leipzig 1922)
LIH	L.W. King, The Letters and Inscriptions of Hammurabi (London 1898-1900)
MC	Mesopotamian Civilizations (Winona Lake 1989ff.)
MEE	Materiali epigrafici di Ebla (Napoli 1979ff.)
Mesopotamia	Mesopotamia. Rivista di Archeologia (Torino 1966f.)
MSL	Materialien zum sumerischen Lexikon (Rome 1937ff.)
N.A.B.U.	Nouvelles Assyriologiques Brèves et Utilitaires (Rouen/Paris 1987ff.)
NG	A. Falkenstein, Die neusumerischen Gerichtsurkunden (München 1956-1957)
OA	Oriens Antiquus. Rivista del Centro per le Antichità e la Storia dell'Arte del Vicino Oriente (Rome 1962ff.)
OIP	Oriental Institute Publications (Chicago 1924ff.)
OrNS	Orientalia. Nova Series (Rome 1932ff.)
PEa	PROTO-Ea (Nippur Recension). In: MSL XIV (Rome 1979) 30-63
PPAC 1	Z. Yang, Sargonic Inscriptions from Adab. The Institute for the History of Ancient Civilisations, Periodic Publications on Ancient Civilisations 1 (Changchun 1989)

PSD	The Sumerian Dictionary of the University Museum of the University of Pennsylvania, edited by Å.W. Sjöberg (Philadelphia 1984ff.)
REC	F. Thureau-Dangin, Recherches sur l'origine de l'écriture cunéiforme (Paris 1898-1899)
RGTC	Répertoire géographique des textes cunéiformes. Beihefte zum Tübinger Atlas des Vorderen Orients, Series B (Wiesbaden 1974ff.)
RIME	The Royal Inscriptions of Mesopotamia, Early Periods (Toronto 1990ff.)
RlA	Reallexikon der Assyriologie (Berlin/Leipzig and Berlin/New York 1932ff.)
SANTAG	SANTAG. Arbeiten und Untersuchungen zur Keilschriftkunde. Herausgegeben von K. Hecker und W. Sommerfeld (Wiesbaden 1990ff.)
SARI	J.S. Cooper, Sumerian and Akkadian Royal Inscriptions I: Presargonic Inscriptions (New Haven 1986)
SAZ	A. Cavigneaux, Die sumerisch-akkadischen Zeichenlisten: Überlieferungsprobleme (Diss. München 1976)
SEL	Studi epigrafici e linguistici sul Vicino Oriente antico (Verona 1984ff.)
SKLy	J. Krecher, Sumerische Kultlyrik (Wiesbaden 1966)
SRU	D.O. Edzard, Sumerische Rechtsurkunden des III. Jahrtausends aus der Zeit vor der III. Dynastie von Ur (München 1968)
St.Pohl	Studia Pohl (Rome 1967ff.)
St.Pohl SM	Studia Pohl: Series Maior (Rome 1969ff.)
Studies Birot	Miscellanea Babylonica. Mélanges offerts à Maurice Birot. Réunis par J.-M. Durand et J.-R. Kupper (Paris 1985)
Studies Borger	*Tikip santakki mala bašmu...* Festschrift für Rykle Borger zu seinem 65. Geburtstag am 24. Mai 1994. Herausgegeben von Stefan M. Maul. Cuneiform Monographs 10 (Groningen 1998)
Studies Diakonoff	Societies and Languages of the Ancient Near East. Studies in Honour of I.M. Diakonoff (Warminster 1982)
Studies Hallo	The Tablet and the Scroll. Near Eastern Studies in honour of William W. Hallo. M.E. Cohen, D.C. Snell, D.B. Weisberg, eds. (Bethesda [MD] 1993)
Studies Matouš	Festschrift Lubor Matouš. Herausgegeben von B. Hruška und G. Komoróczy (Budapest 1978)
Studies Sjöberg	DUMU-E$_2$-DUB-BA-A. Studies in Honor of Åke W. Sjöberg. Edited by H. Behrens, D. Loding and M.T. Roth. Occasional

	Publications of the Samuel Noah Kramer Fund 11 (Philadelphia 1989)
Studies Tadmor	Ah, Assyria ... Studies in Assyrian History and Ancient Near Eastern Historiography, presented to Hayim Tadmor. M. Cogan and I. Eph'al, eds. (Jerusalem 1991)
Sumer	Sumer. A Journal of Archaeology and History in Iraq. The Republiq of Iraq. Directorate General of Antiquities (Baghdad 1945ff.)
TCS	Texts from Cuneiform Sources (Locust Valley [New York] 1966ff.)
ThŠH	J. Klein, Three Šulgi Hymns. Sumerian Royal Hymns Glorifying King Šulgi of Ur (Ramat-Gan 1981)
TMH(NF)	Texte und Materialien der Frau Prof. Hilprecht Collection of Babylonian Antiquities (Neue Folge: Leipzig, Berlin 1932ff.)
TUAT	O. Kaiser (ed.), Texte aus der Umwelt des Alten Testaments (Gütersloh 1982ff.)
UET	Ur Excavations, Texts (London 1928ff.)
UGASL	G.J. Selz, Untersuchungen zur Götterwelt des altsumerischen Stadtstaates von Lagaš. Occasional Publications of the Samuel Noah Kramer Fund 13 (Philadelphia 1995)
UVB	Uruk, Vorläufiger Bericht über die von dem Deutschen Archäologischen Institut und der Deutschen Orient-Gesellschaft aus Mitteln der Deutschen Forschungsgemeinschaft unternommenen Ausgrabungen in Uruk-Warka (Berlin 1930ff.)
VA	Siglum of the *V*orderasiatische *A*bteilung of the Vorderasiatisches Museum, Berlin
VS	Vorderasiatische Schriftdenkmäler der Königlichen/Staatlichen Museen zu Berlin (Leipzig, Berlin 1907ff.)
WO	Die Welt des Orients (Wuppertal, Stuttgart and Göttingen 1947ff.)
WVDOG	Wissenschaftliche Veröffentlichungen der Deutschen Orient-Gesellschaft (Leipzig, Berlin 1901ff.)
Xenia	Xenia. Konstanzer Althistorische Vorträge und Forschungen (W. Schuller ed., Konstanz 1981ff.)
YOS	Yale Oriental Series, Babylonian Texts (New Haven 1915ff.)
ZA(NF)	Zeitschrift für Assyriologie (Leipzig, Berlin, Straßburg 1886ff.; Neue Folge: Berlin/Leipzig, Berlin, Berlin/New York 1924ff.)

LIST OF TEXTS

The number of each text is accompanied by the original publication of the copy reproduced in this book and by its most recent edition.

I. Royal Inscriptions

1. CT XXI, pl. 3, No. 90015 (brick); D.R. Frayne, RIME 3/2, 69ff. ('Ur-Nammu E3/2.1.1.33')
2. YOS IX 14 (clay nail); D.O. Edzard, RIME 3/1, 113 ('Gudea E3/1.1.7.8')
3. CT XXI, pl. 2, No. 90009 (brick); D.R. Frayne, RIME 3/2, 25f. ('Ur-Nammu E3/2.1.1.4')
4. VS I 22, VA 57 (brick); D.O. Edzard, RIME 3/1, 156 ('Gudea E3/1.1.7.64')
5. CT XXI, pl. 36, No. 90289 (brick); D.O. Edzard, RIME 3/1, 154f. ('Gudea E3/1.1.7.62')
6. CT XXI, pl. 37, No. 90288 (brick); D.O. Edzard, RIME 3/1, 120f. ('Gudea E3/1.1.7.18')
7. OIP 14 33 (brick); D.O. Edzard, RIME 3/1, 135f. ('Gudea E3/1.1.7.37')
8. VS I 23, VA 3129 (brick); D.O. Edzard, RIME 3/1, 141f. ('Gudea E3/1.1. 7.44')
9. VS 1 21, VA 55 (brick); D.O. Edzard, RIME 3/1, 130f. ('Gudea E3/1.1.7.31')
10. FT II, pl. XXXIX, TG 2429 (stone tablet); D.O. Edzard, RIME 3/1, 109f. ('Gudea E3/1.1.7.4')
11. CIRPL 34, Ent. 18 (door socket); H. Steible, FAOS 5/1, 221f. ('Entemena 18')
12. CIRPL 1, Urn. 3 (copper nail); H. Steible, FAOS 5/1, 79f. ('Urnanše 2')
13. CIRPL 35, Ent. 22 (door socket); H. Steible, FAOS 5/1, 222f. ('Entemena 22')
14. CIRPL 36, Ent. 27 (door socket); H. Steible, FAOS 5/1, 227f. ('Entemena 27')
15. DC I, pl. XLVI; photo: DC II, pl. 31bis, 3 (brick); H. Steible, FAOS 5/1, 182ff. ('Enannatum I. 2')
16. DC I, pl. XLV (brick); H. Steible, FAOS 5/1, 165ff. ('E'annatum 22')
17. CIRPL 59, Ukg. 17 (clay olive); H. Steible, FAOS 5/1, 338f. ('Uru'inimgina 17')
18. CIRPL 56, Ukg. 10 (stone tablet); H. Steible, FAOS 5/1, 326ff. ('Uru'-inimgina 10')
19. CIRPL 45, En.II 1 (door socket); H. Steible, FAOS 5/1, 273f.

20. CIRPL 36, Ent. 26 (door socket); H. Steible, FAOS 5/1, 226f. ('Entemena 26')
21. CIRPL 32, Ent. 1 (diorite statue); H. Steible, FAOS 5/1, 211ff. ('Entemena 1')
22. DC I, pl. VI-VII (diorite statue, "petite statue debout"); D.O. Edzard, RIME 3/1, 29f. ('Gudea E3/1.1.7.StA')
23. DC I, pl. XVI-XVII (diorite statue, "statue dite aux épaules étroites"); D.O. Edzard, RIME 3/1, 38ff. ('Gudea E3/1.1.7.StC')
24. DC I, pl. XVII-XIX (diorite statue, "statue colossale"); D.O. Edzard, RIME 3/1, 40ff. ('Gudea E3/1.1.7.StD')
25. DC I, pl. XXIII-XXV (diorite statue, "l'architecte à la règle"); D.O. Edzard, RIME 3/1, 46ff. ('Gudea E3/1.1.7.StF')
26. DC I, pl. XVIII (diorite statue, "petite statue assise, acéphale"); D.O. Edzard, RIME 3/1, 50f. ('Gudea E3/1.1.7.StH')
27. UVB 10, pl. 28 (door socket); D.R. Frayne, RIME 3/2, 262ff. ('Amar-Suena E3/2.1.3.16')
28. LIH 58 (shaft); D.R. Frayne, RIME 4, 347ff. ('Ḫammu-rāpi E4.3.6.12')
29. UET 8 84 (cone head); D.R. Frayne, RIME 4, 278f. ('Rīm-Sîn I E4.2.14.6')

II. Legal Documents

30. OIP 14 192 (clay tablet); Z. Yang, PPAC 1, 119-120; 346-347 (loan of silver)
31. TMHNF 1/2 24 (clay tablet); N. Schneider, OrNS 8 (1939) 62 (loan of silver)
32. JCS 8 (1954) 46 (clay tablet); A. Falkenstein, NG 2, 1f. (marriage decree)
33. DV 3/II 293 (clay tablet); G.J. Selz, FAOS 15/1, 521f. (purchase of slaves and workers)
34. DV 3/II 17 (clay tablet); D.O. Edzard, SRU, 93f. (purchase of a cult singer)
35. TMH 5 216 (clay tablet); D.O. Edzard, SRU, 127 (guarantee)
36. TMHNF 1/2 259 (clay tablet); A. Falkenstein, NG 2, 212f. (record of an oath)
37. NG III, pl. 2 (clay tablet); A. Falkenstein, NG 2, 27f. (suit for breach of betrothal promise)
38. ITT 3/2, pl. 21, 5279 (clay tablet); A. Falkenstein, NG 2, 159ff. (claim of property and a slave; liberation of the daughters of this slave)
39. ZA 55 (1962) 71 (clay tablet); for this controversial document see S. Greengus, HUCA 40-41 (1969-1970) 33-44; J. van Dijk, OrNS 39 (1970) 99-102; Å. Sjöberg, ibid. 92; M. Roth, JAOS 103 (1983) 278 ad 24; H. Lutzmann, TUAT 1

(1982) 198; J.-M. Durand, AEM I/1, 525 b); C. Wilcke, Xenia 32 (1992) 70[25] (decree of divorce)

III. Economic Documents

40. VS 14/1 44 (clay tablet); J. Bauer, AWL, 281f. (delivery of fodder)
41. VS 14/1 128 (clay tablet); J. Bauer, AWL, 324 (delivery of animal products for a festival)
42. VS 14/1 35 (clay tablet); J. Bauer, AWL, 289f. (account of sheep and goats)
43. VS 14/1 145 (clay tablet); J. Bauer, AWL, 296f. (purchase and branding of a steer)
44. VS 14/1 157 (clay tablet); J. Bauer, AWL 452ff. (offering of beer to the gods)

1

i ii

1 1

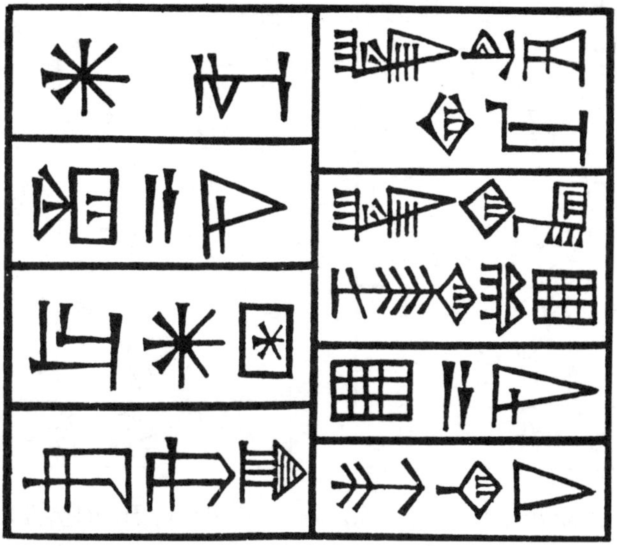

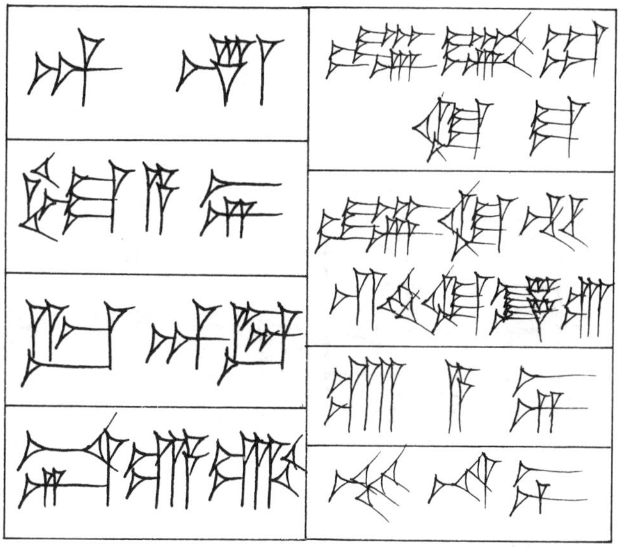

^{d}inanna / nin-a-ni / ur-^{d}nammu / nita-kala-ga / lugal-uri$_{5}$ (ŠEŠ.AB)^{ki}-ma / lugal-ki-en-gi-ki-uri-ke$_{4}$ / é-a-ni / mu-na-dù

2

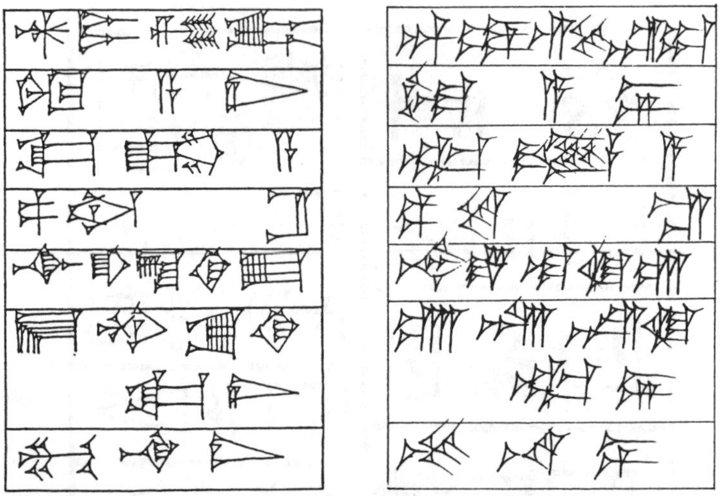

^{d}dumu-zi-abzu(ZU.AB) / nin-a-ni / gù-dé-a / énsi(PA.TE.SI)- / lagaš(ŠIR.BUR.LA)^{ki}-ke$_{4}$ / é-g̃ír-su^{ki}-ka-ni / mu-na-dù

3

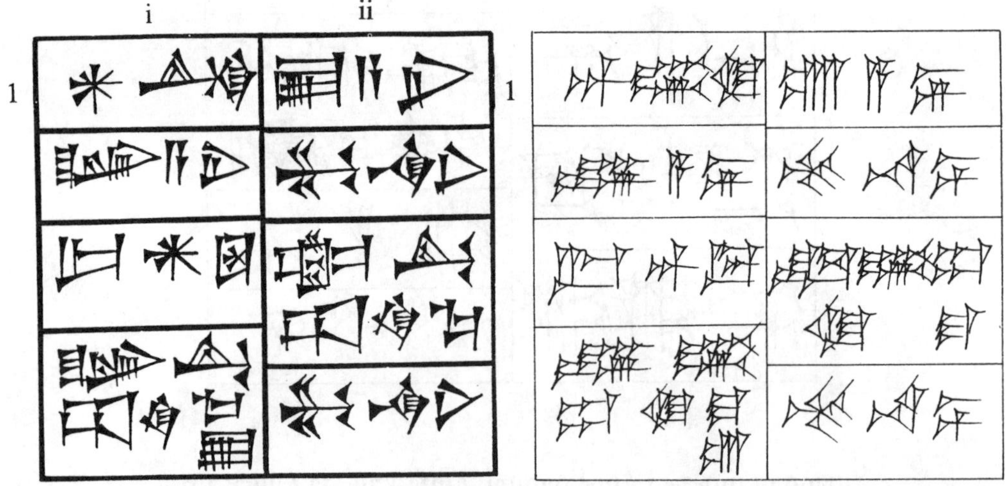

^{d}nanna(ŠEŠ.KI) / lugal-a-ni / ur-^{d}nammu / lugal-uri$_{5}$(ŠEŠ.AB)^{ki}-ma-ke$_{4}$ / é-a-ni / mu-na-dù / bàd-uri$_{5}$(ŠEŠ.AB)^{ki}-ma / mu-na-dù

4

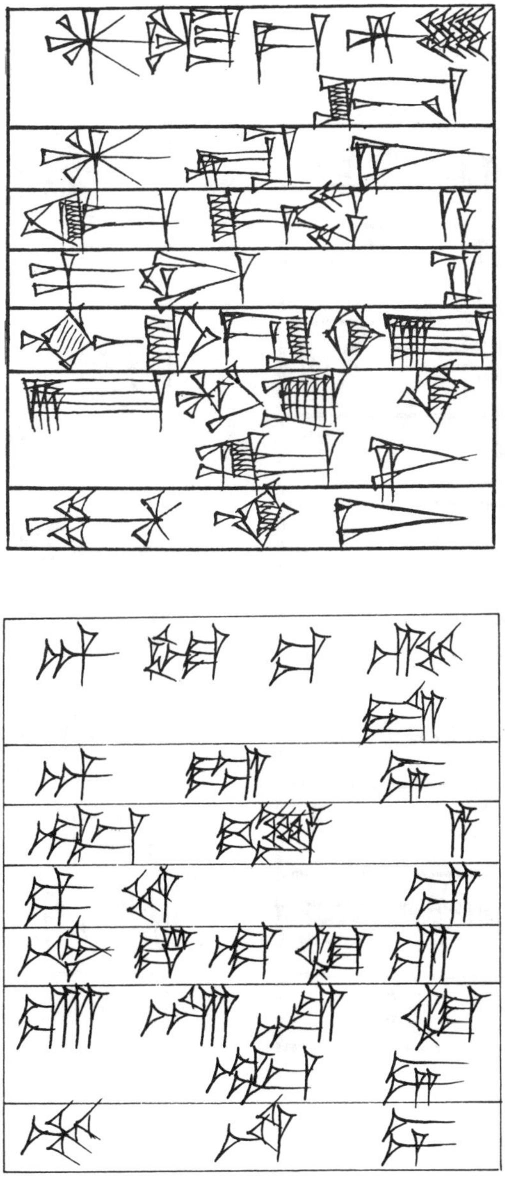

^{d}nin-ĝiš-zi-da / diĝir-ra-ni / gù-dé-a / énsi(PA.TE.SI)- / lagaš(ŠIR.BUR.LA)^{ki}-ke$_{4}$ / é-ĝír-su^{ki}-ka-ni / mu-na-dù

5

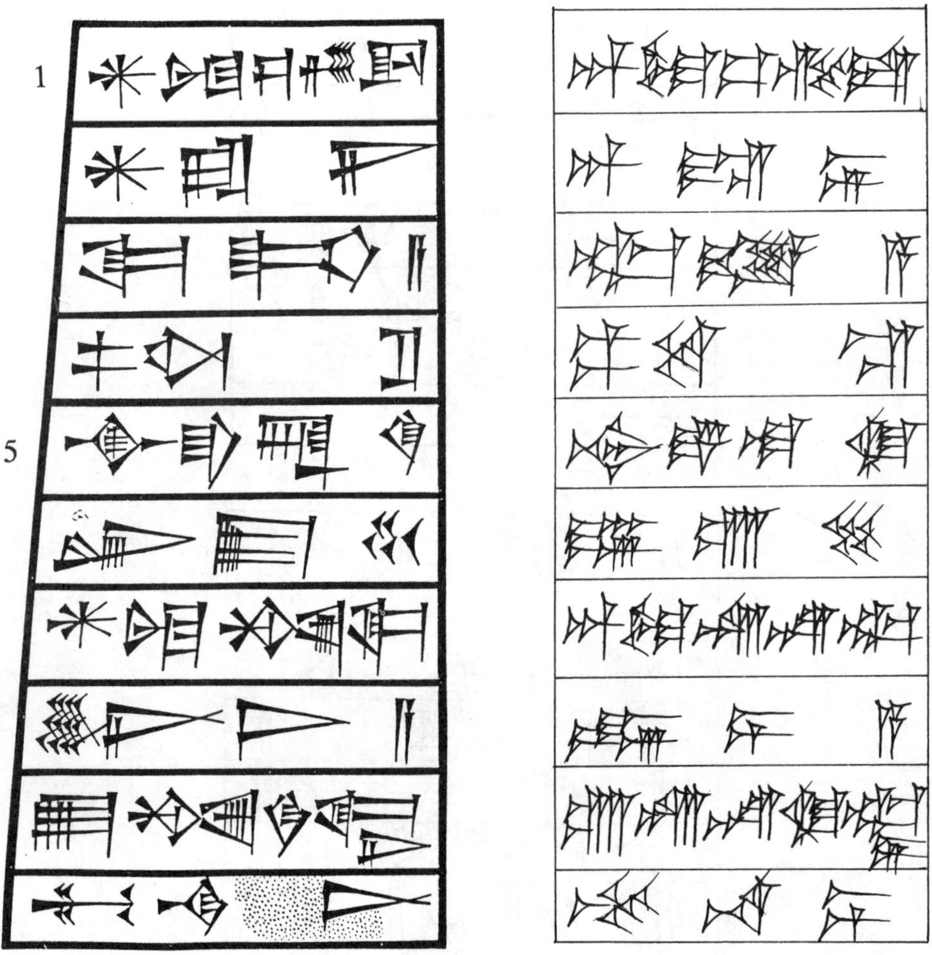

6

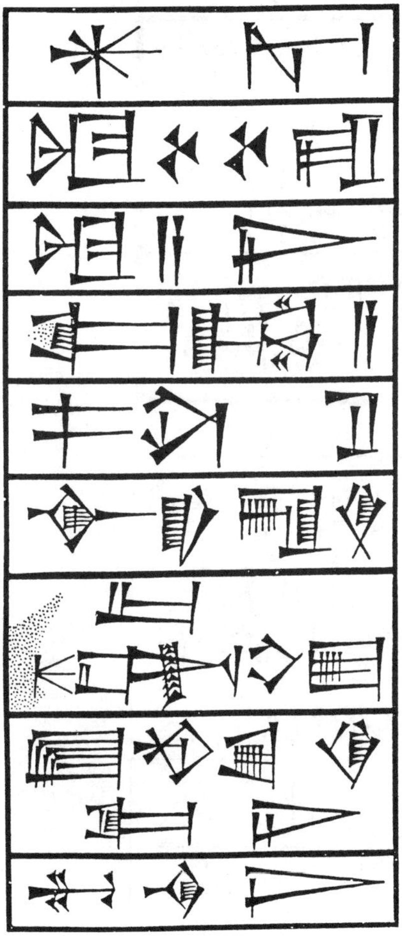

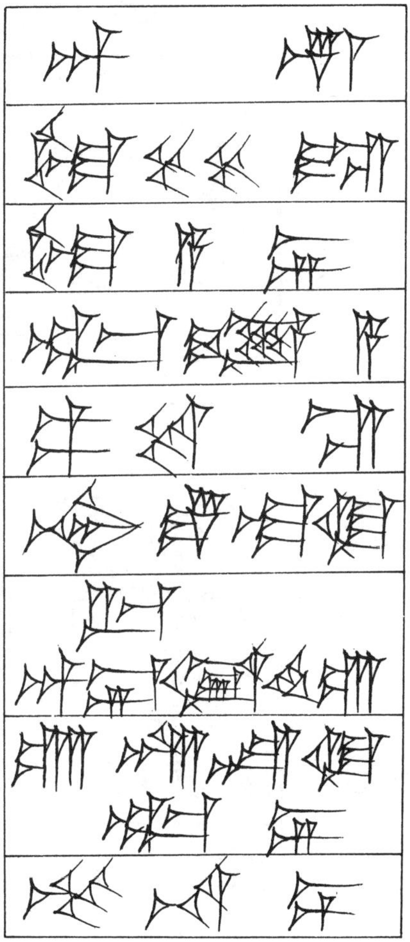

^{d}inanna / nin-kur-kur-ra / nin-a-ni / gù-dé-a / énsi(PA.TE.SI)-/ lagaš(ŠIR.BUR.LA)^{ki} / ur-$^{\ulcorner d \urcorner}$g̃á-tùm-du$_{10}$-ke$_{4}$ / é-g̃ír-su^{ki}-ka-ni / mu-na-dù

7

i ii

1 1

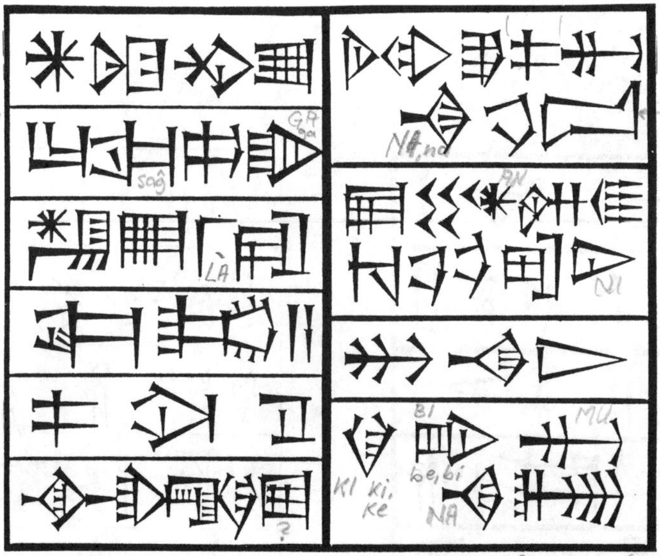

5

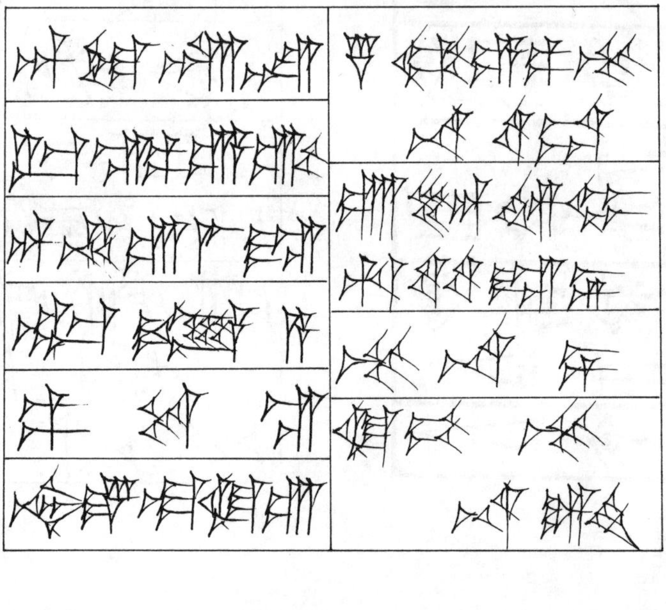

^{d}nin-ĝír-su / ur-saĝ-kala-ga- / ^{d}en-líl-lá-ra / gù-dé-a / énsi(PA.TE.SI)-/ lagaš(ŠIR.BUR.LA)^{ki}-ke$_{4}$ / níĝ-ul-e pa mu-na-è(UD.DU) / é-ninnu-^{d}anzu(IM.MI)^{mušen}-bábbar-ra-ni / mu-na-dù / ki-bi mu-na-gi$_{4}$

8

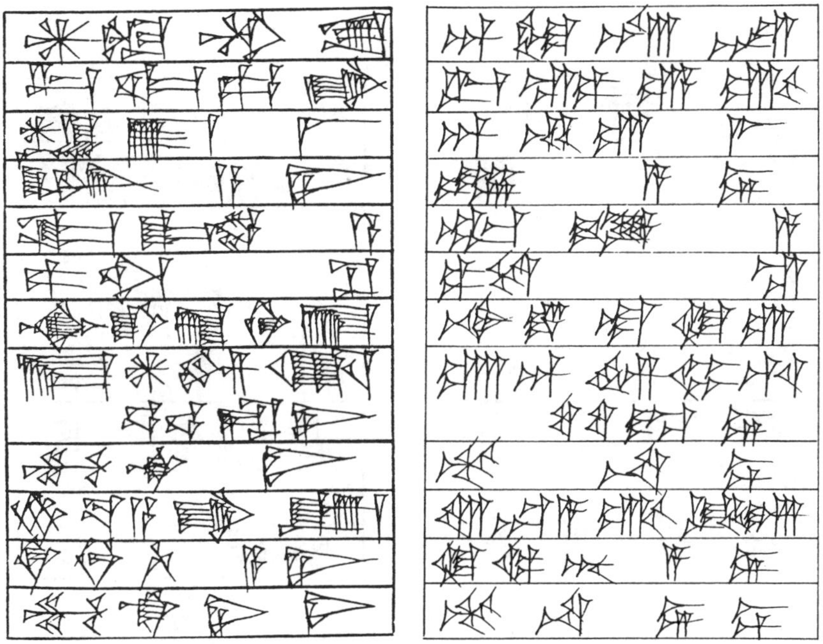

9

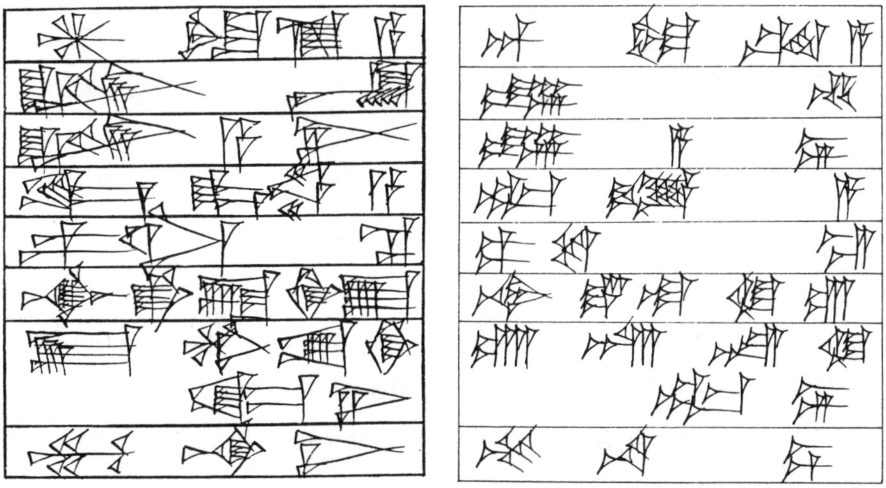

10

obv.
1
5

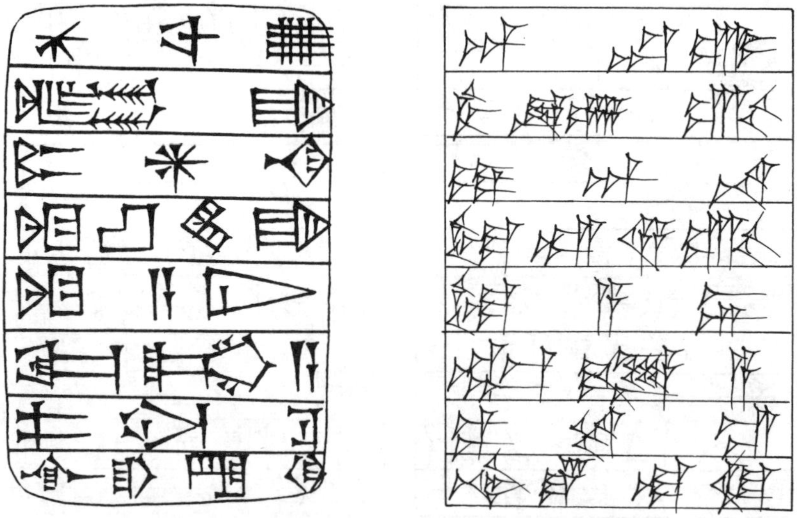

rev.
1
5

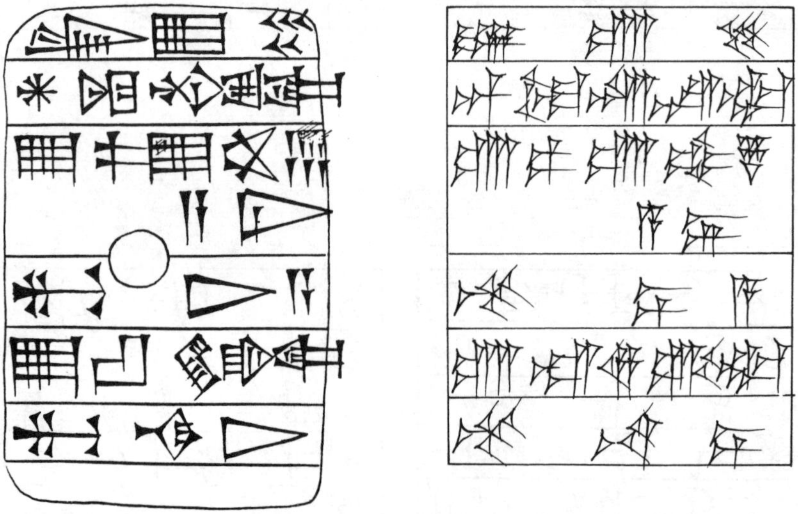

^{d}ba-U$_{2}$ / munus-sa$_{6}$-ga / dumu-an-na / nin-iri-kù-ga / nin-a-ni / gù-dé-a / énṣi(PA.TE.SI)- / lagaš(ŠIR.BUR.LA)^{ki} / lú é-ninnu- / ^{d}nin-g̃ír-su-ka / é-g̃idru é-ub-⸢imin⸣-a-ni / mu-dù-a / é-iri-kù-ga-ka‹-ni› / mu-na-dù

11

1 5
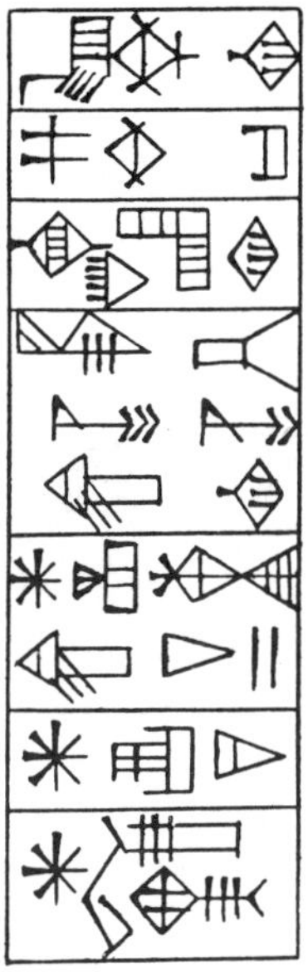

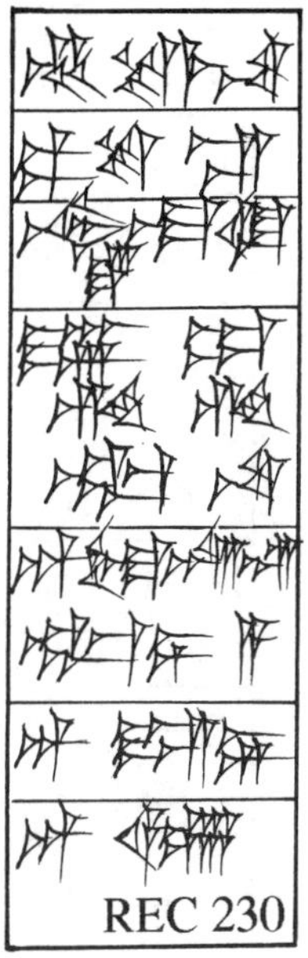

en-te:me-na / énsi(PA.TE.SI)- / lagaš(ŠIR.BUR.LA)^{ki} / lú èš-gi-gi-gù-na- / ^{d}nin-g̃ír-sú-ka dù-a / dig̃ir-ra-ni / ^{d}šul-utul$_{12}$

12

i 1

ii 1
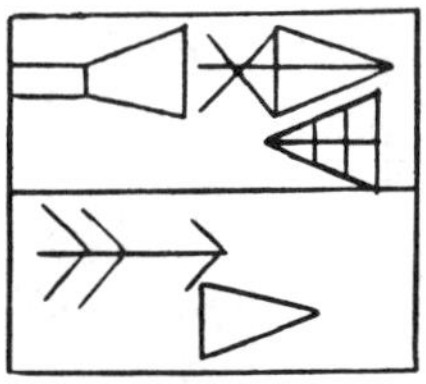

13

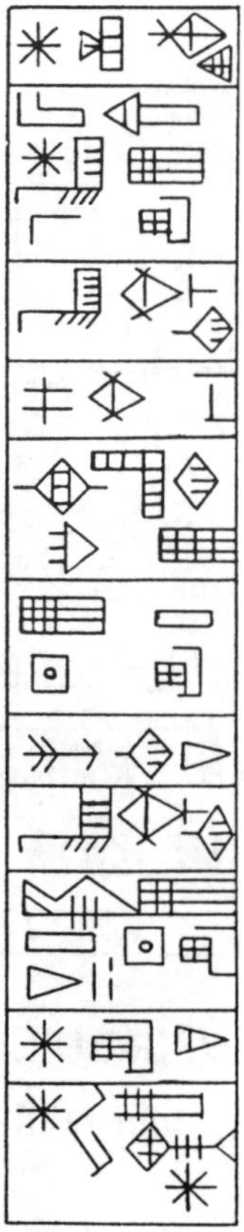

^{d}nin-ĝír-sú

ur-saĝ-
^{d}en-líl-
lá-ra

en-te:me-na

énsi(PA.TE.SI)-

lagaš(ŠIR.BUR.LA)^{ki}
-ke$_4$

é-^{ĝiš}gígir-ra

mu-na-dù

en-te:me-na

lú-é-
^{ĝiš}gígir-ra
dù-a

diĝir-ra-ni

^{d}šul-utul$_{12}$-am$_6$

14

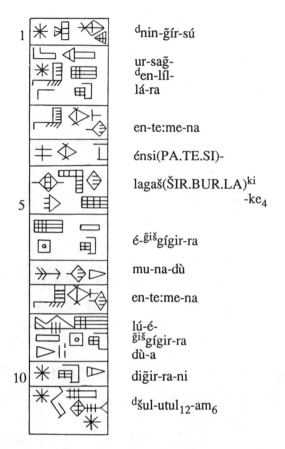

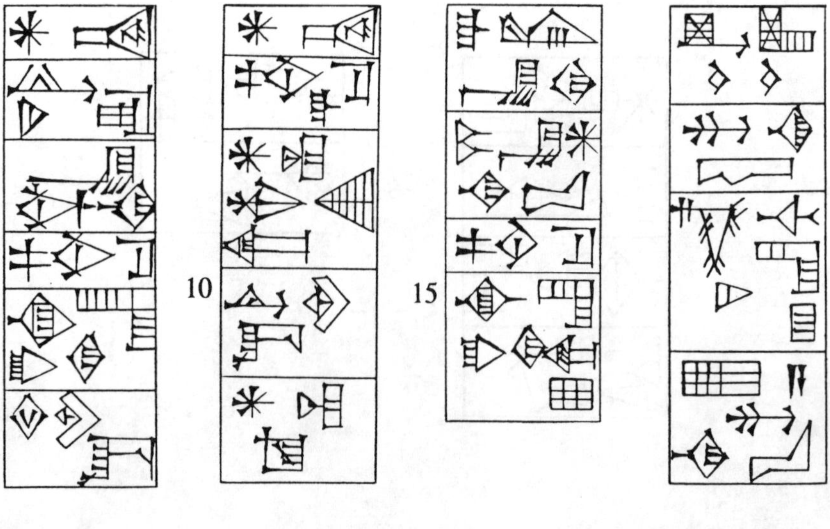

15

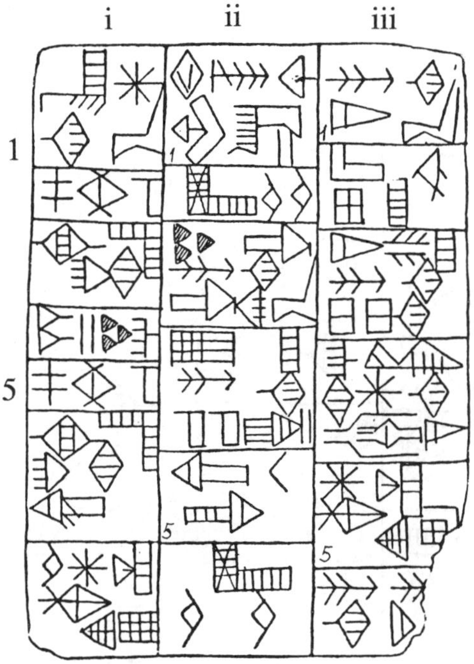

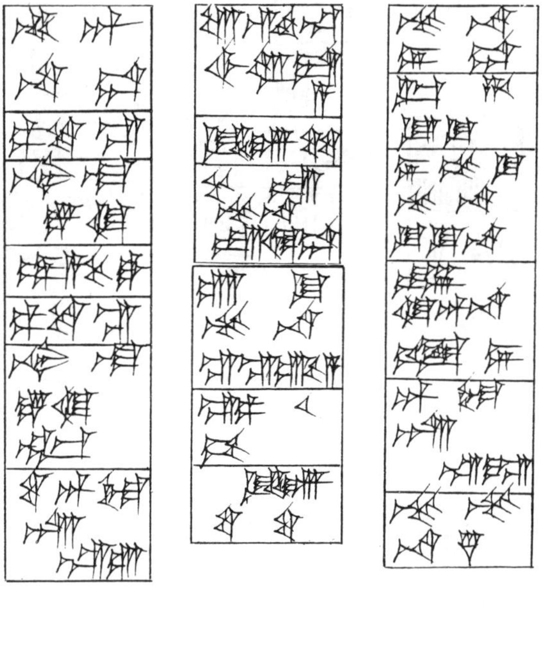

16

i ii iii

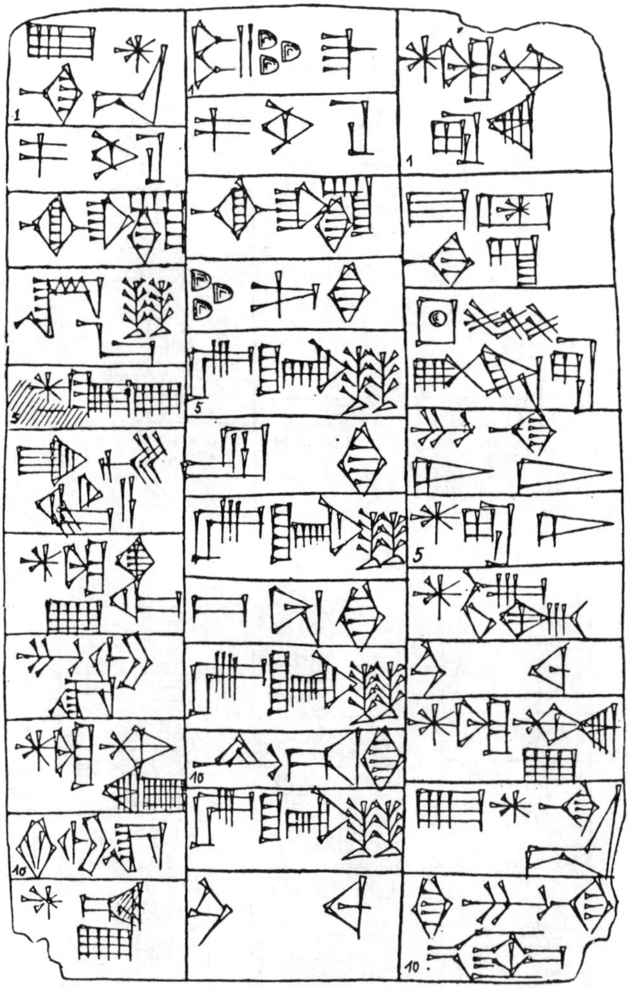

17

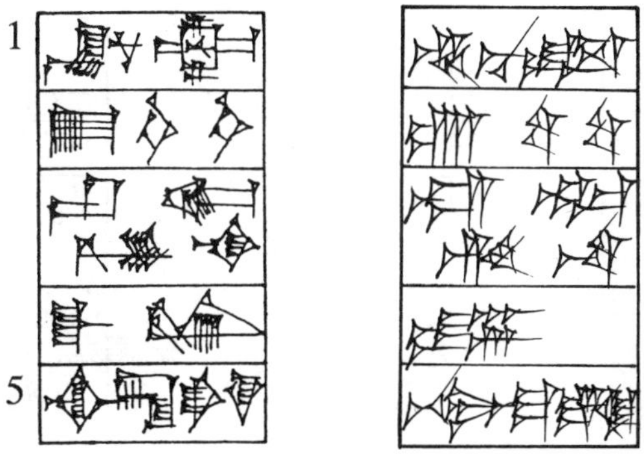

18

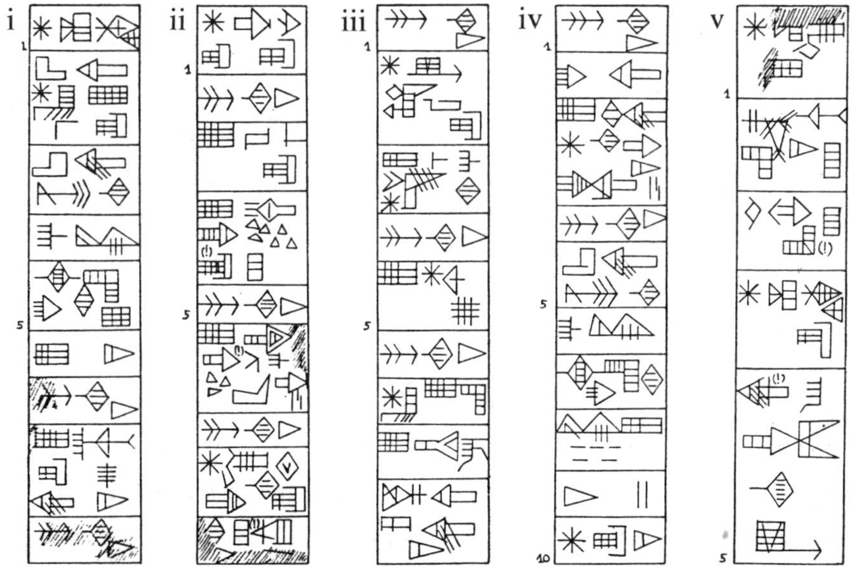

19

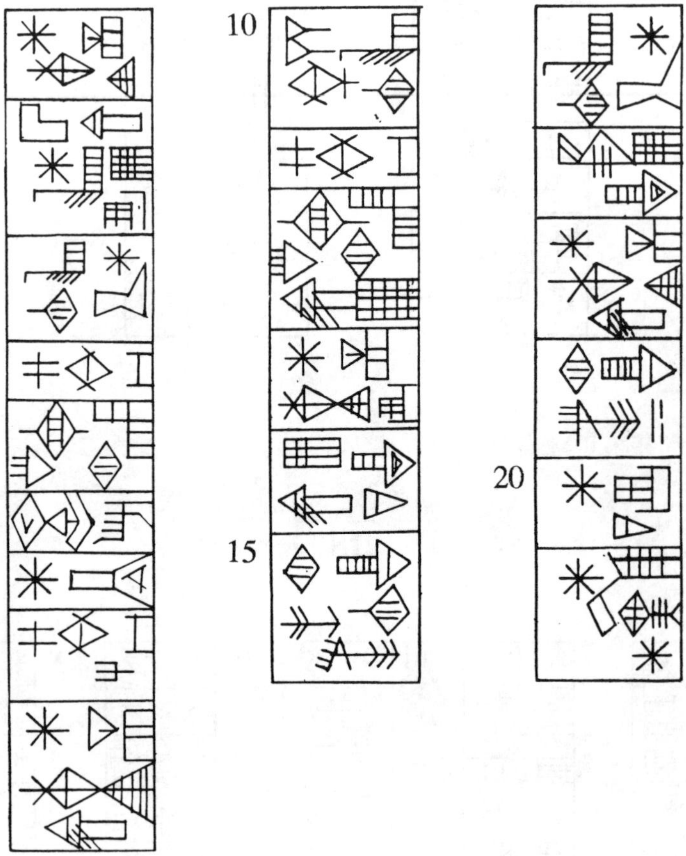

^{d}nin-g̃ír-sú / ur-sag̃-^{d}en-líl-ra / en-an-na-túm / énsi(PA.TE.SI)- / *(5)* lagaš(ŠIR.BUR.LA)^{ki} / šà-pà-da- / ^{d}nanše / énsi-gal- / ^{d}nin-g̃ír-sú-ka / *(10)* dumu-en-te:me-na- / énsi(PA.TE.SI)- / lagaš(ŠIR.BUR.LA)^{ki}-ka-ke$_{4}$ / ^{d}nin-g̃ír-sú-ra / é-bàppir-ka-ni / *(15)* ki-bi mu-na-gi$_{4}$ / en-an-na-túm / lú é-bàppir- / ^{d}nin-g̃ír-sú-ka / ki-bi gi$_{4}$-a / *(20)* dig̃ir-ra-ni / ^{d}šul-utul$_{12}$-am$_{6}$

20

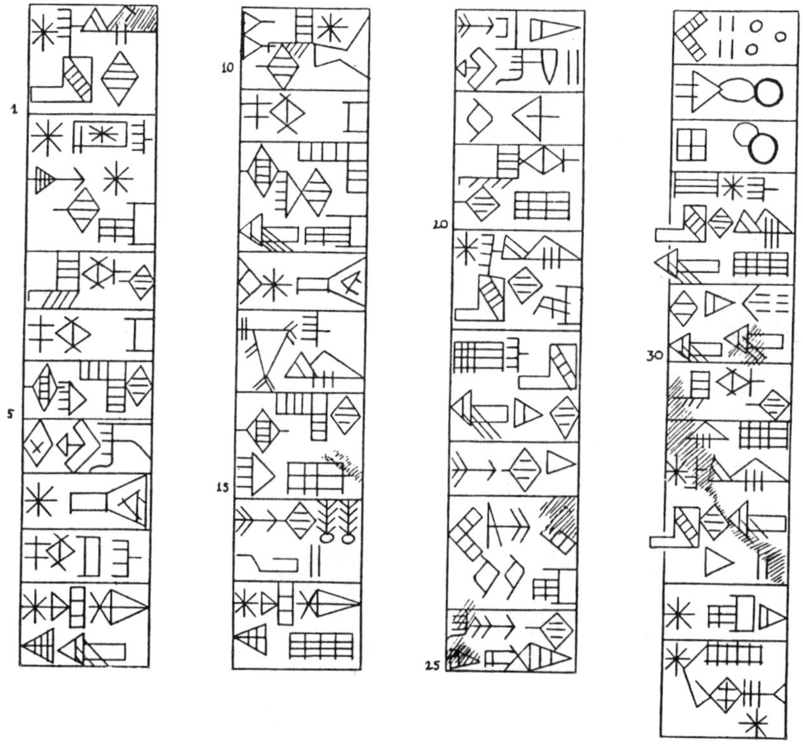

^{d}lugal-uru$_{x}$(URUxKAR$_{2}$)^{ki} / ^{d}ama-ušumgal-an-na-ra / en-te:me-na / énsi(PA.TE.SI)- / *(5)* lagaš(ŠIR.BUR.LA)^{ki} / šà-pà-da- / ^{d}nanše / énsi(PA.TE.SI)-gal- / ^{d}nin-g̃ír-sú-ka / *(10)* dumu-en-an-na-túm / énsi (PA.TE.SI)- / lagaš(ŠIR.BUR.LA)^{ki}-ka-ra / u$_{4}$ ^{d}nanše / nam-lugal- / *(15)* lagaš(ŠIR.BUR.LA)^{ki}-sa / mu-na-šúm-ma-a / ^{d}nin-g̃ír-sú-ke$_{4}$ / mu e-ni-pà-da-a / u$_{4}$-ba / *(20)* en-te:me-na-ke$_{4}$ / ^{d}lugal-uru$_{x}$(URUxKAR$_{2}$)^{ki}-ra / é-gal-uru$_{x}$(URUxKAR$_{2}$)^{ki}-ka-ni / mu-na-dù / kù-sig$_{17}$ ⸢kù⸣-bábbar-ra / *(25)* šu mu-na-ni-tag / kù-za-gìn / gu$_{4}$-20 / udu-20 / kisal-^{d}lugal-uru$_{x}$ (URUxKAR$_{2}$)^{ki}-ka-ke$_{4}$ / *(30)* sá ì-mi-du$_{11}$-du$_{11}$ / en-te:me-na / [l]ú é-^{d}lugal-uru$_{x}$(URUxKAR$_{2}$)^{ki}-ka dù-a / dig̃ir-ra-ni / ^{d}šul-utul$_{12}$-am$_{6}$

21

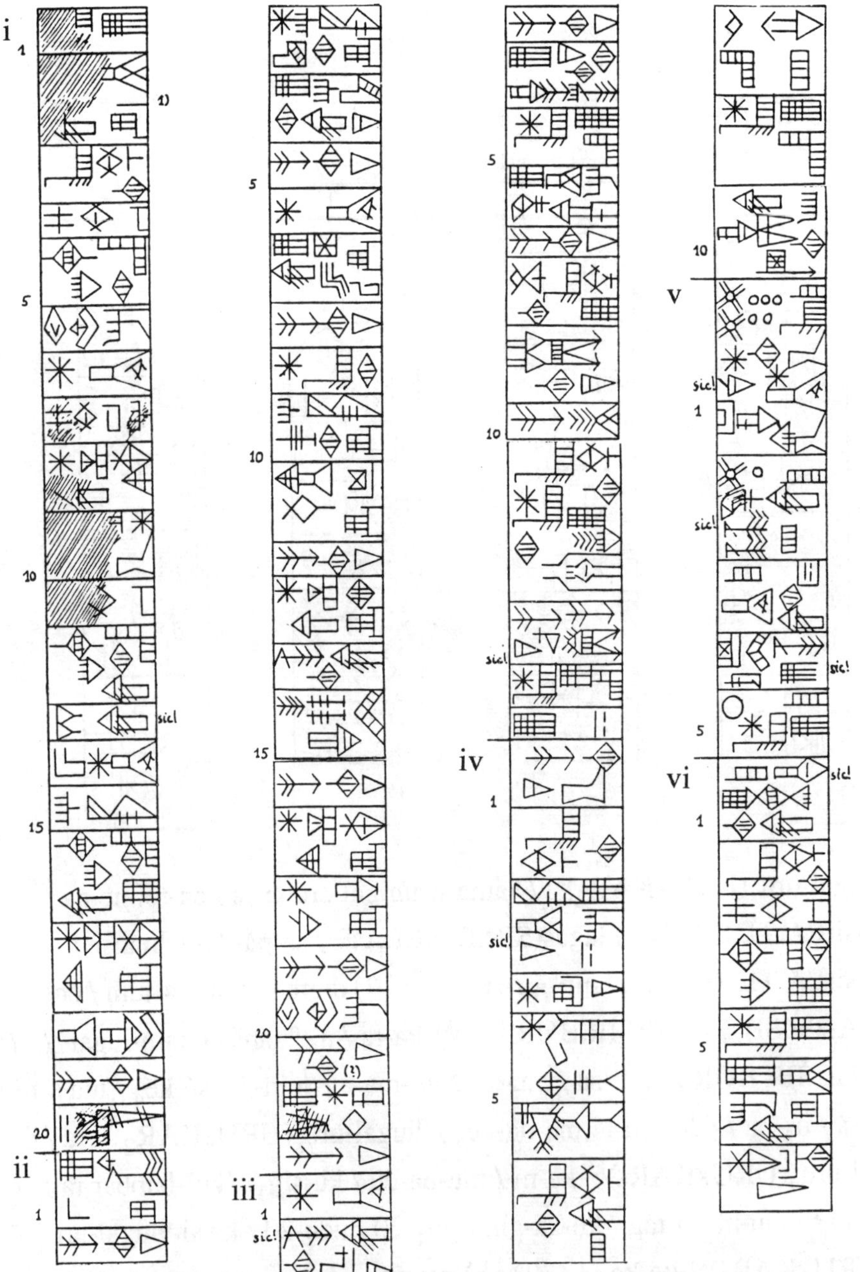

(1) This line is to be read [E_2]-ad-[da]-⌜ka⌝-ra, cf. vi 6.

22

r. sh.

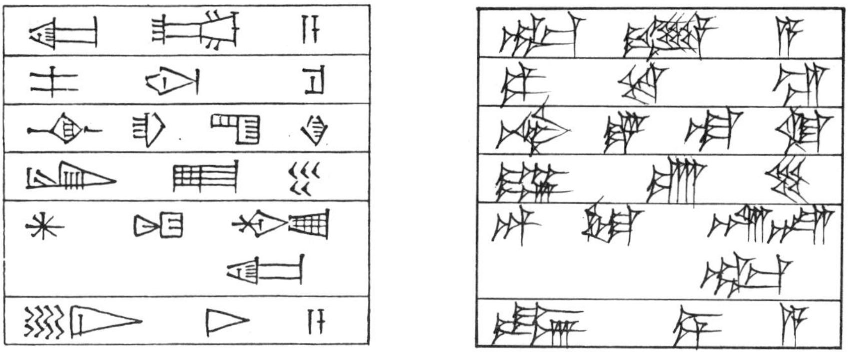

i 1

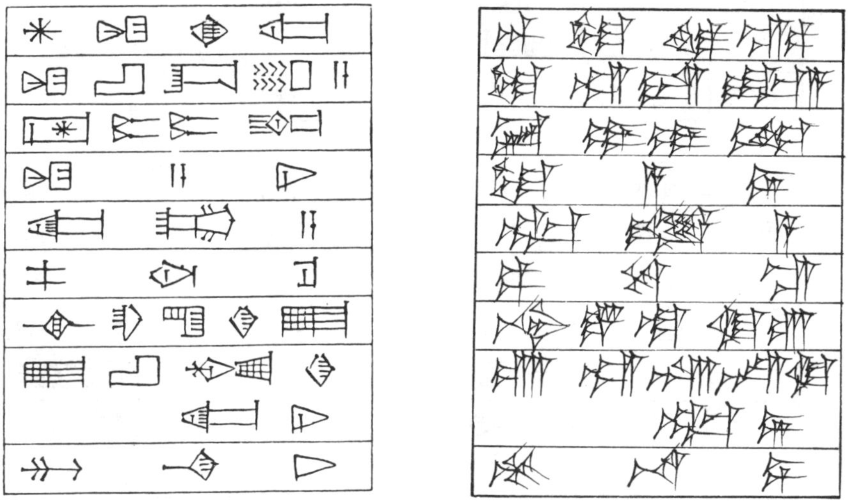

ii 1

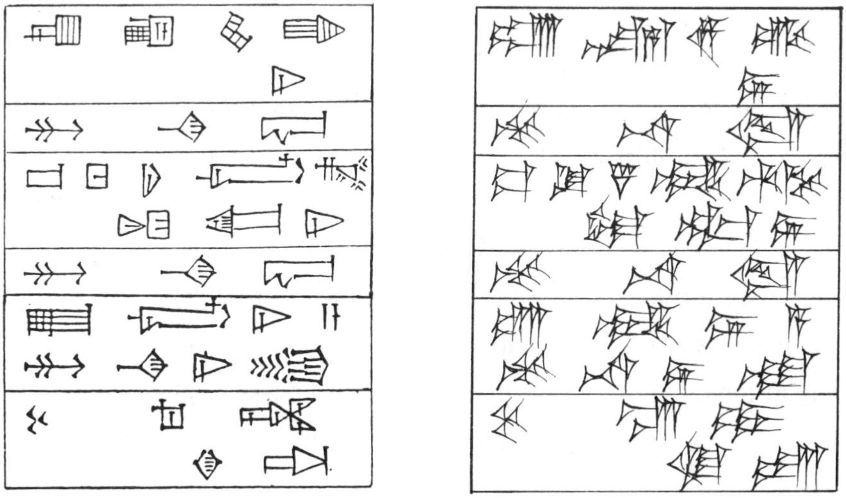

22 ctd.

iii 1 ... 5

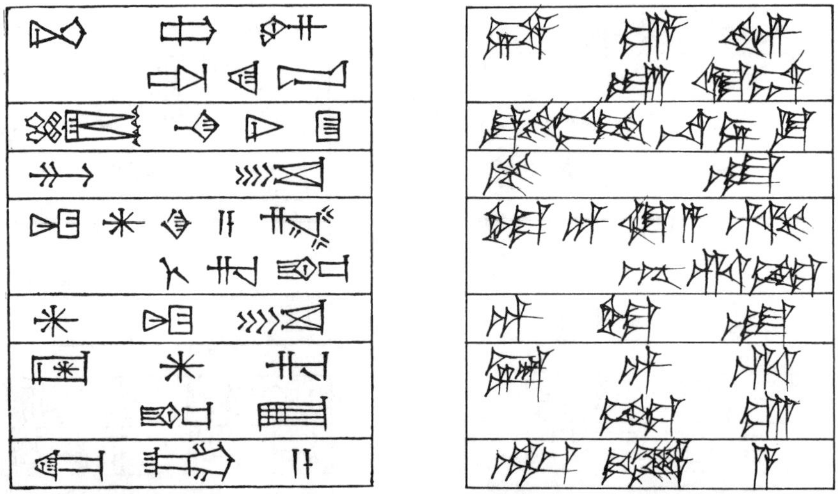

iv 1

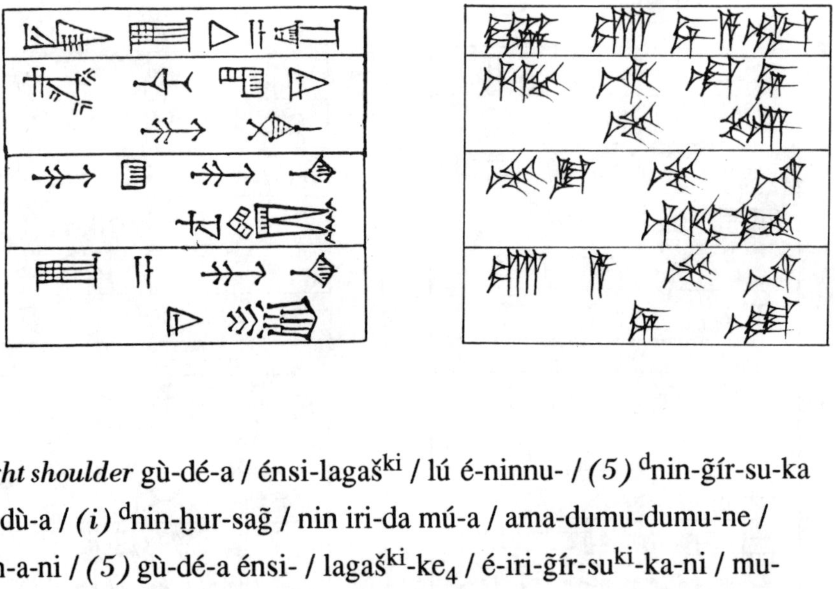

right shoulder gù-dé-a / énsi-lagaš^{ki} / lú é-ninnu- / *(5)* ^{d}nin-g̃ír-su-ka in-dù-a / *(i)* ^{d}nin-ḫur-sag̃ / nin iri-da mú-a / ama-dumu-dumu-ne / nin-a-ni / *(5)* gù-dé-a énsi- / lagaš^{ki}-ke$_{4}$ / é-iri-g̃ír-su^{ki}-ka-ni / mu-na-dù / *(ii)* DUB.ŠEN(= REC 429)-kù-ga-ni / mu-na-dím / $^{g̃iš}$dúr-g̃ar-maḫ-nam-nin-ka-ni / mu-na-dím / *(5)* é-maḫ-ni-a mu-na-ni-ku$_{4}$ / kur-má-gan^{ki}-ta / *(iii)* ^{na4}esi im-ta-e$_{11}$ alan-na-ni-šè / mu-tu / nin an-ki-a nam-tar-re-dè / *(5)* ^{d}nin-tu / ama-dig̃ir-re-ne-ke$_{4}$ / gù-dé-a / *(iv)* lú-é-dù-a-ka / nam-ti-la-ni mu-sù / mu-šè mu-na-sa$_{4}$ / é-a mu-na-ni-ku$_{4}$

23

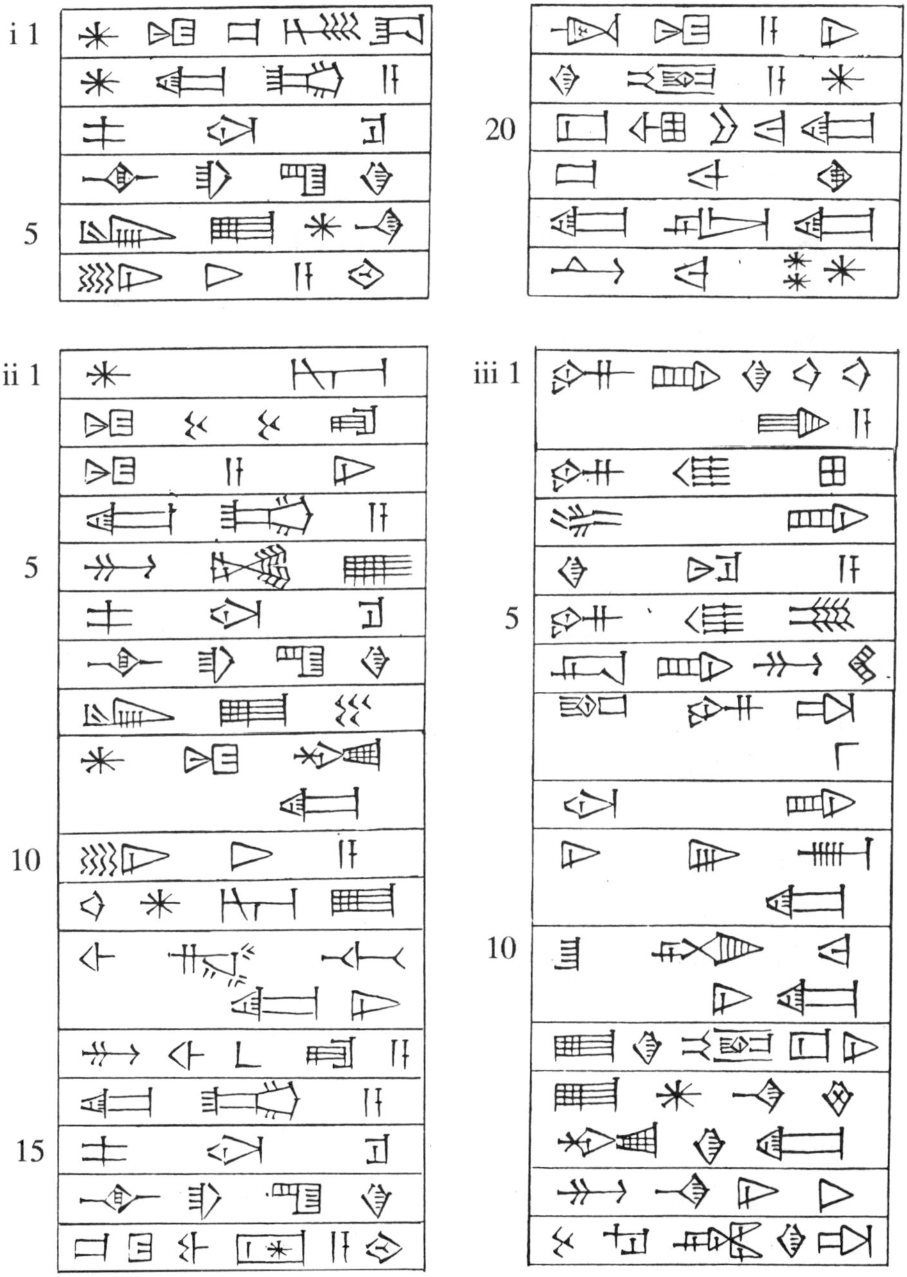

23 ctd.

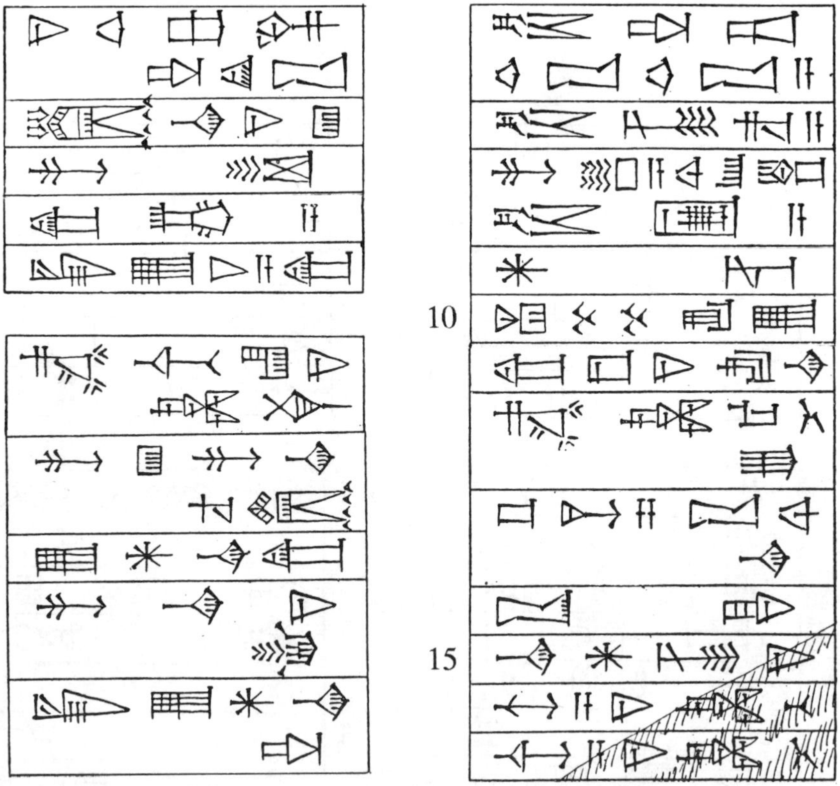

(i) ^{d}nin-g̃iš-zi-da / dig̃ir-gù-dé-a / énsi- / lagaš^{ki} / *(5)* lú é-an-na / in-dù-a-kam / *(ii)* ^{d}inanna / nin-kur-kur-ra / nin-a-ni / gù-dé-a *(5)* mu-gi$_{16}$-sa / énsi- / lagaš^{ki} / lú é-ninnu- / ^{d}nin-g̃ír-su-ka / *(10)* in-dù-a / u$_{4}$ ^{d}inanna-ke$_{4}$ / igi-nam-ti-ka-ni / mu-ši-bar-ra-a / gù-dé-a / *(15)* énsi- / lagaš^{ki} / g̃éštu-dag̃al-a-kam / úrdu nin-a-ni / ki-ág̃-àm / *(20)* g̃á-ù-šub-ba-ka / g̃iš ba-ḫur / ka-al-ka / urin ba-mul / *(iii)* im-bi ki-dadag-ga-a / im-mi-lu / sig$_{4}$-bi / ki-sikil-a / *(5)* im-mi-du$_{8}$ / uš-bi mu-kù / izi im-ta-lá / temen-bi / ì-ir-nun-ka / *(10)* šu-tag ba-ni-du$_{11}$ / é-ki-ág̃-g̃á-ni / é-an-na šà-g̃ír-su^{ki}-ka / mu-na-ni-dù / kur-má-gan-^{ki}-ta / *(15)* ^{na4}esi im-ta-e$_{11}$ / alan-na-ni-šè / mu-tu / gù-dé-a / lú-é-dù-a-ka / *(iv)* nam-ti-la-ni ḫé-sù / mu-šè mu-na-sa$_{4}$ / é-an-na-ka / mu-na-ni-ku$_{4}$ / *(5)* lú é-an-na-ta / íb-ta-ab-è-è-a / íb-zi-re-a / mu-sar-a-ba šu bí-ib-uru$_{12}$-a / ^{d}inanna / *(10)* nin-kur-kur-ra-ke$_{4}$ / sag̃-g̃á-ni unken-na / nam ḫé-ma-KU$_{5}$-e / $^{g̃iš}$gu-za-gub-ba-na / suḫuš-bi / *(15)* na-an-gi-⸢né⸣ / numun-a-ni ⸢ḫé-til⸣ / bal-⸢a-ni ḫé-ku$_{5}$⸣

24

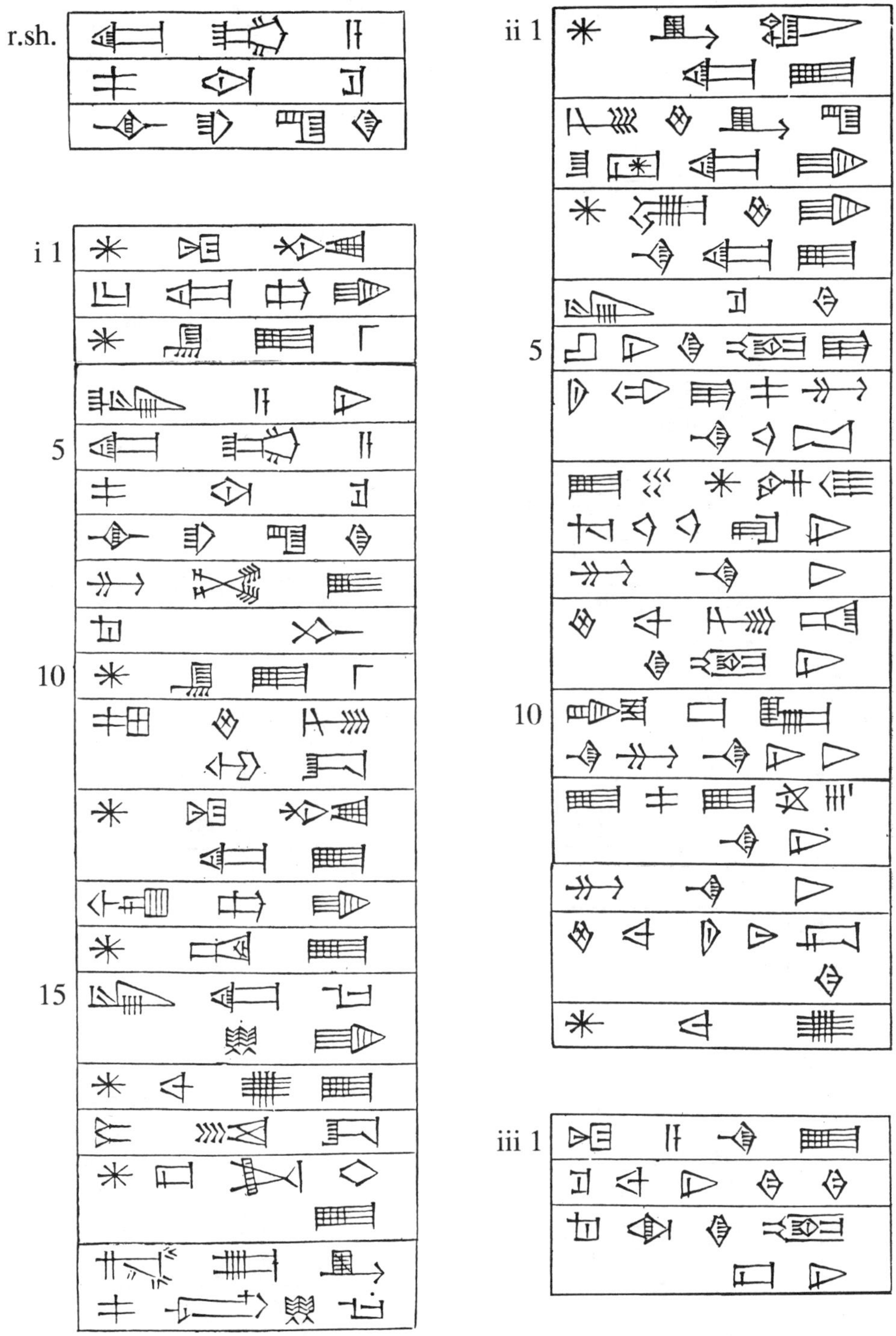

24 ctd.

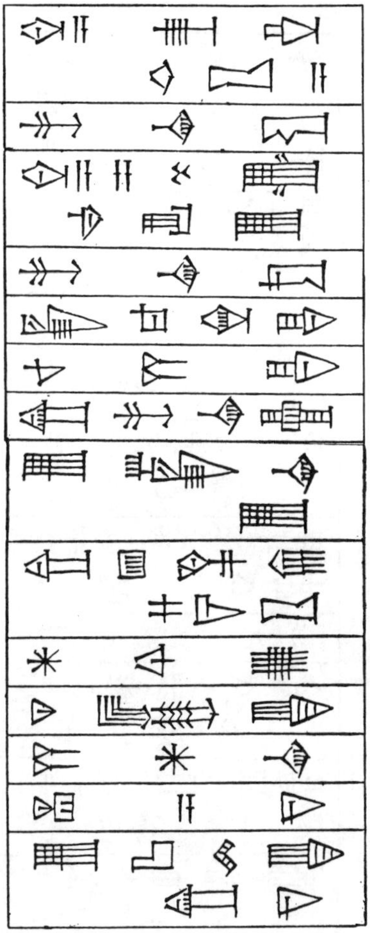

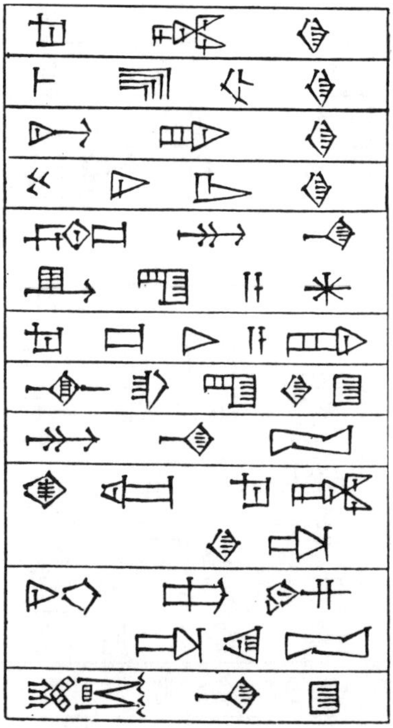

iv 1

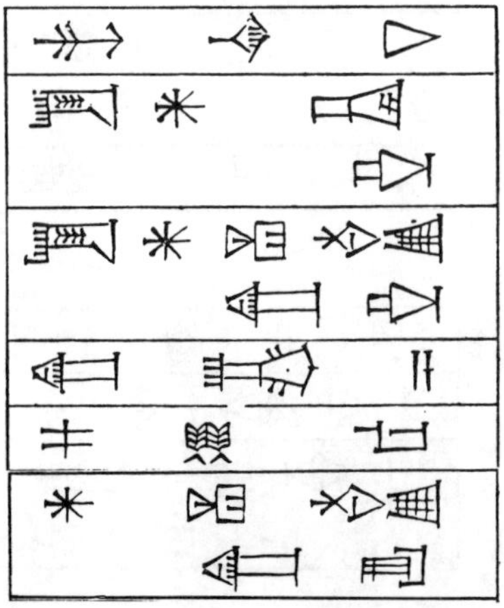

v 1

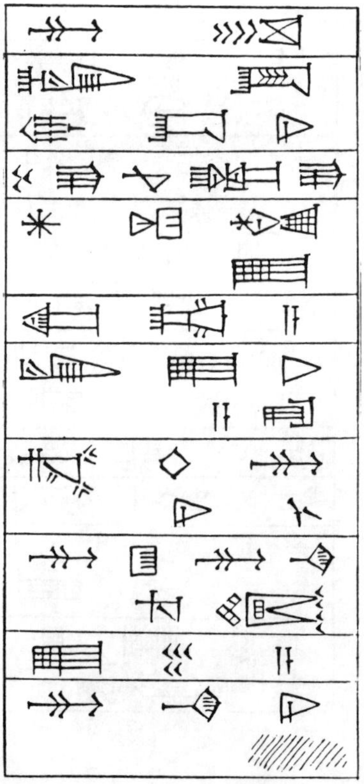

25

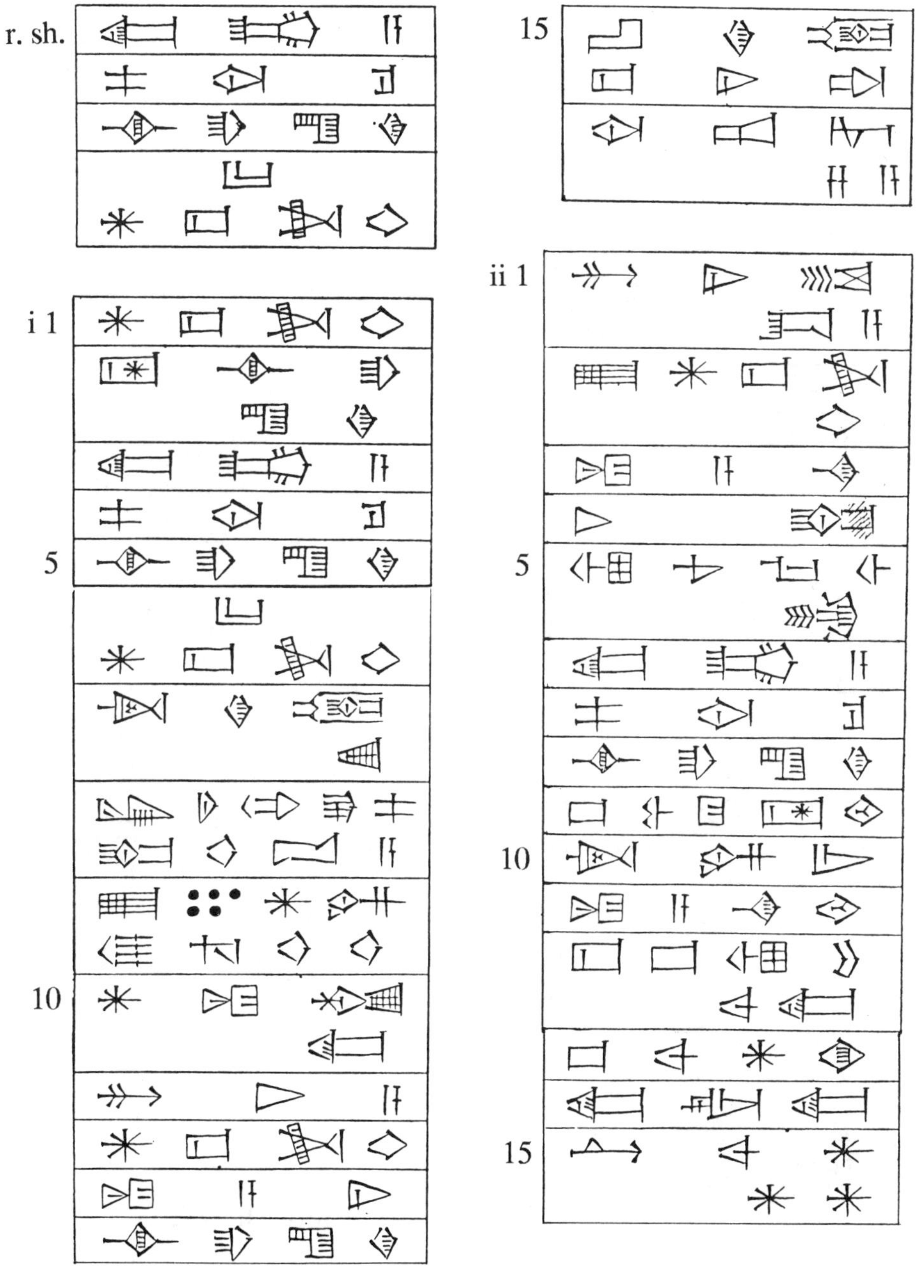

25 ctd.

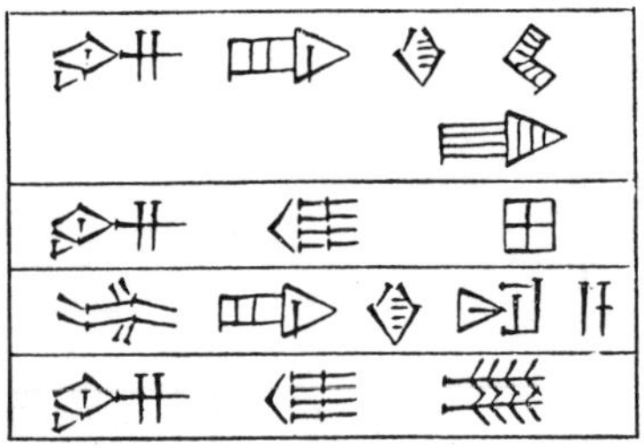

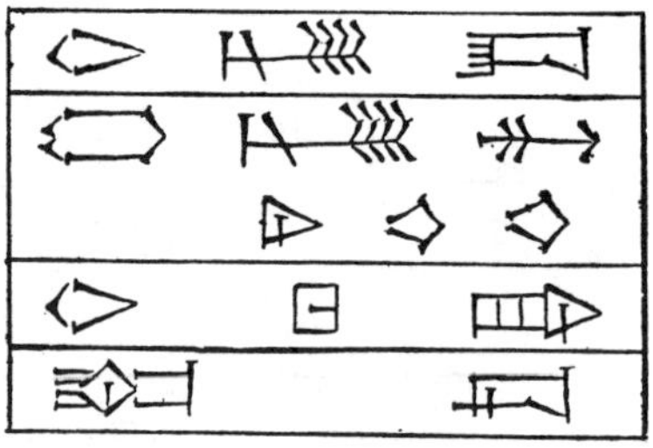

iii 1, 5, 10, 15

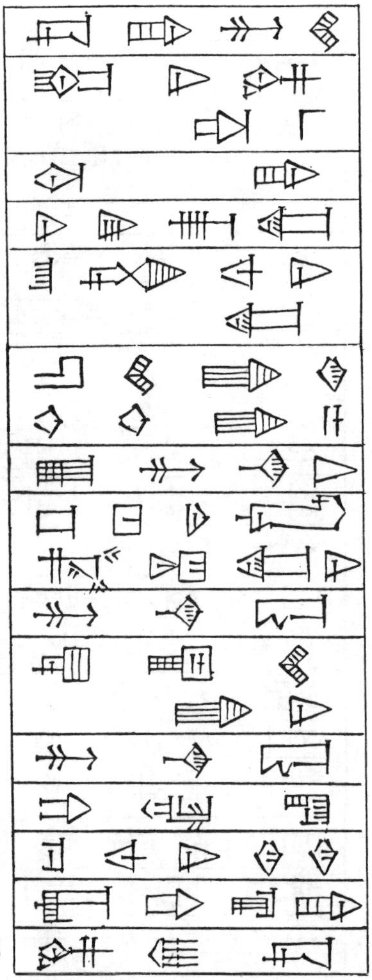

iv 1, 5, 10

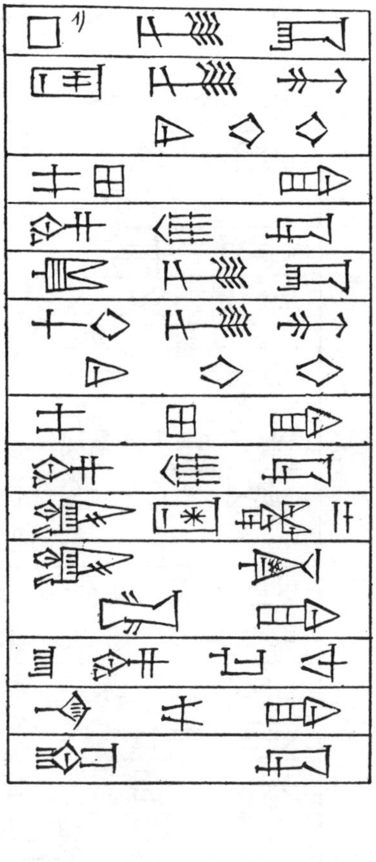

1) Collation shows a clear

26

i 1

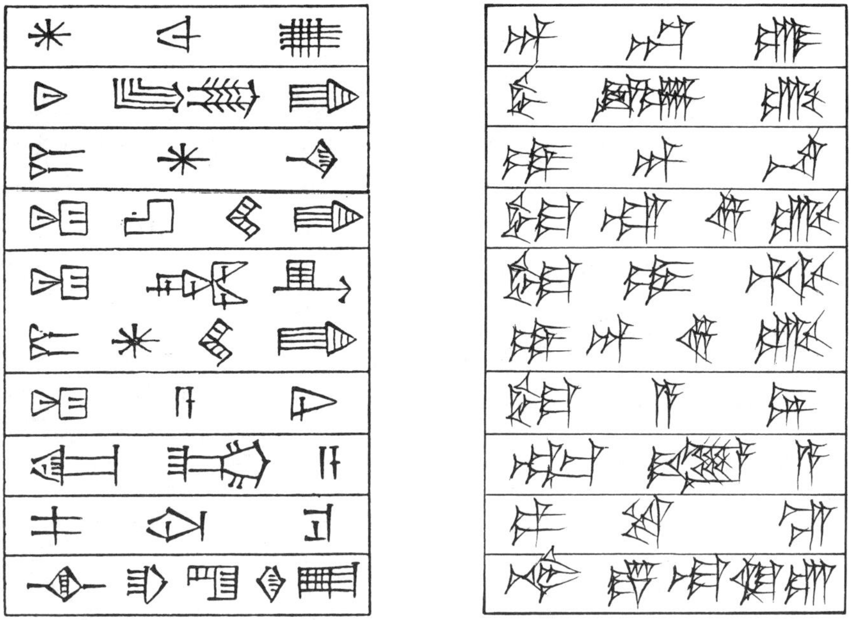

ii 1

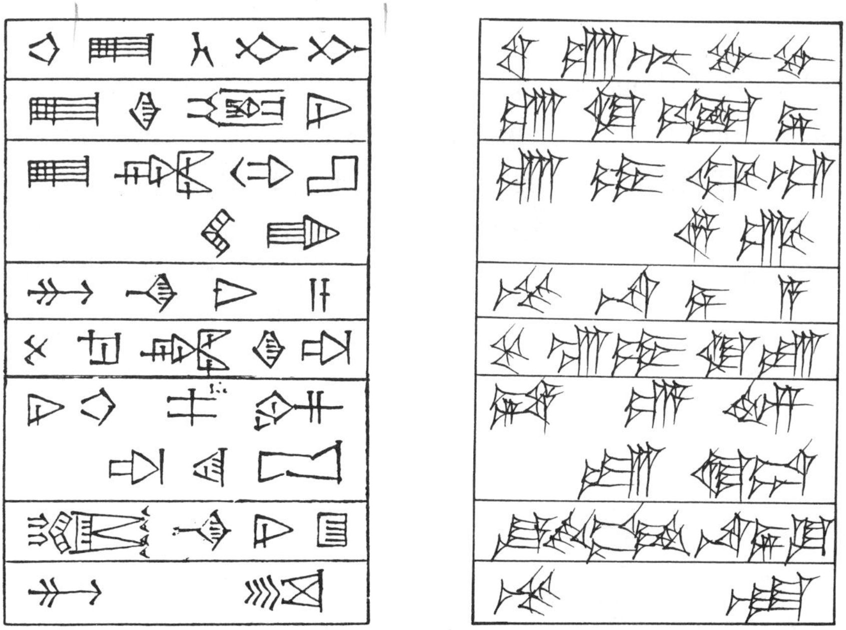

26 ctd.

iii 1

5

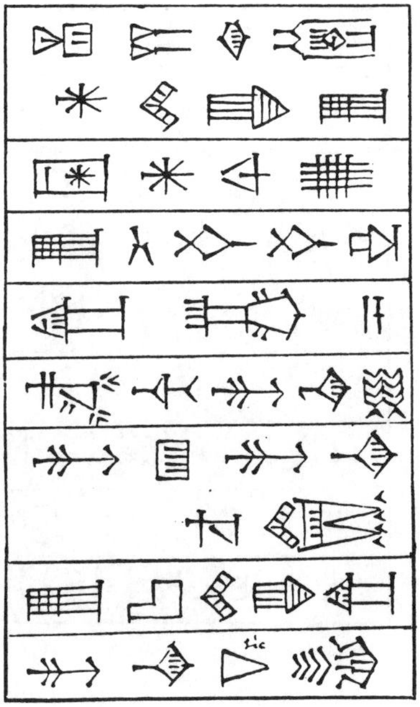

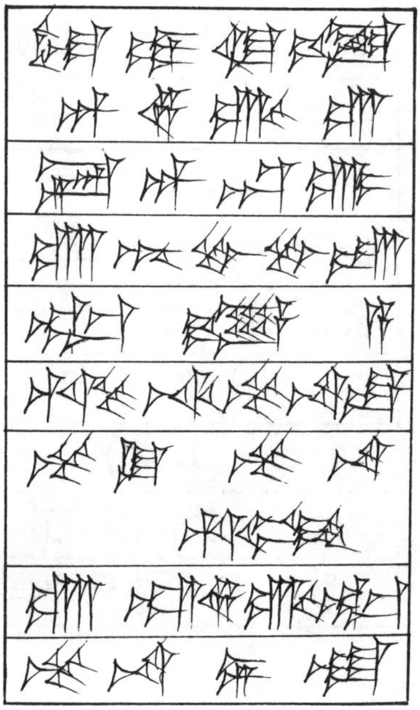

(i) ^{d}ba-U$_2$ / munus-sa$_6$-ga / dumu-an-na / nin-iri-kù-ga / *(5)* nin-ḫé-g̃ál dumu-an-kù-ga / nin-a-ni / gù-dé-a / énsi- / lagaš^{ki}-ke$_4$ / *(ii)* u$_4$ é-TAR-sír-sír / é-ki-ág̃-ni / é ḫé-du$_7$-iri-kù-ga / mu-na-dù-a / *(5)* kur-má-gan^{ki}-ta / ^{na4}esi$^{!}$ (=PA) im-ta-e$_{11}$ / alan-na-ni-šè / mu-tu *(iii)* nin dumu-ki-ág̃-an-kù-ga-ke$_4$ / ama ^{d}ba-U$_2$ / é-TAR-sír-sír-ta / gù-dé-a / *(5)* nam-ti mu-na-šúm / mu-šè mu-na-sa$_4$ / é-iri-kù-ga-ka / mu-na-ni$^{!}$ (=GAG)-ku$_4$

27

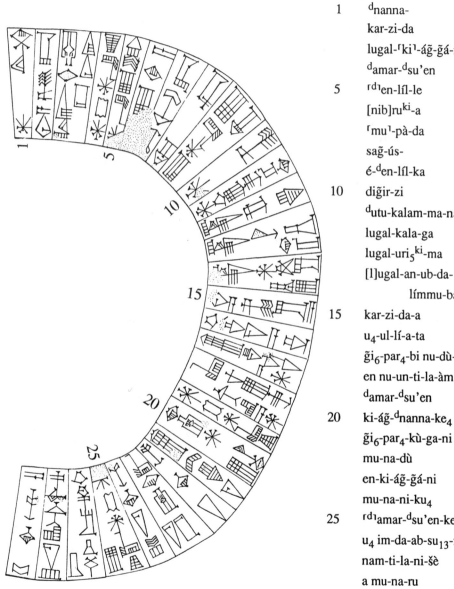

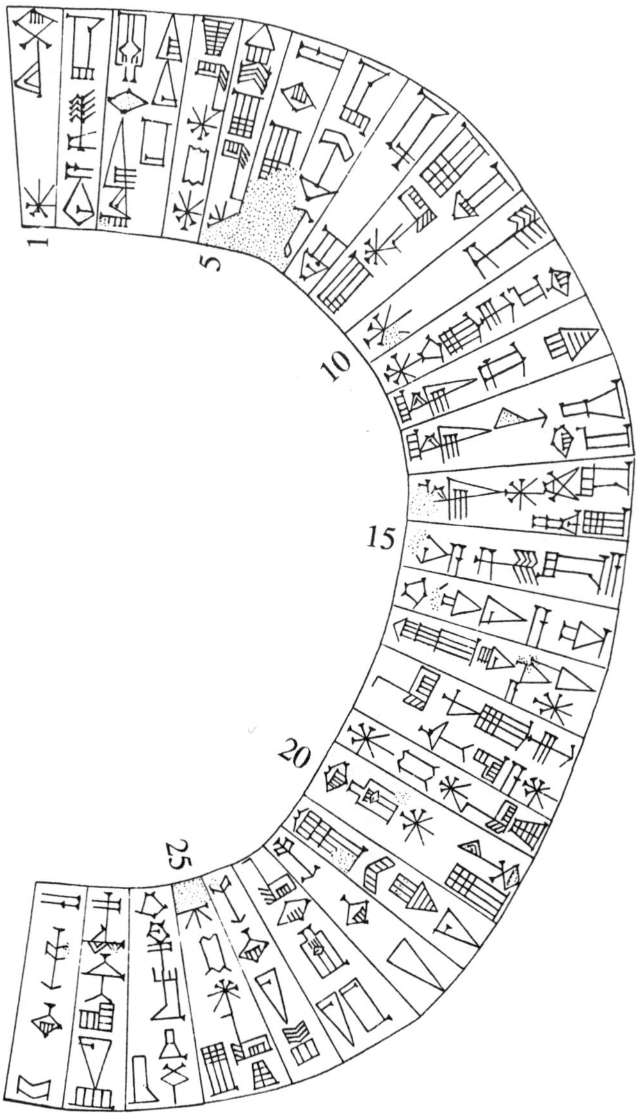

^{d}nanna-
kar-zi-da
lugal-⌜ki⌝-áĝ-ĝá-ni-ir
^{d}amar-^{d}su'en
⌜d⌝en-líl-le
[nib]ru^{ki}-a
⌜mu⌝-pà-da
saĝ-ús-
é-^{d}en-líl-ka
diĝir-zi
^{d}utu-kalam-ma-na
lugal-kala-ga
lugal-uri$_{5}$^{ki}-ma
[l]ugal-an-ub-da-
límmu-ba-ke$_{4}$
kar-zi-da-a
u$_{4}$-ul-lí-a-ta
ĝi$_{6}$-par$_{4}$-bi nu-dù-àm
en nu-un-ti-la-àm
^{d}amar-^{d}su'en
ki-áĝ-^{d}nanna-ke$_{4}$
ĝi$_{6}$-par$_{4}$-kù-ga-ni
mu-na-dù
en-ki-áĝ-ĝá-ni
mu-na-ni-ku$_{4}$
⌜d⌝amar-^{d}su'en-ke$_{4}$
u$_{4}$ im-da-ab-su$_{13}$-re$_{6}$
nam-ti-la-ni-šè
a mu-na-ru

28

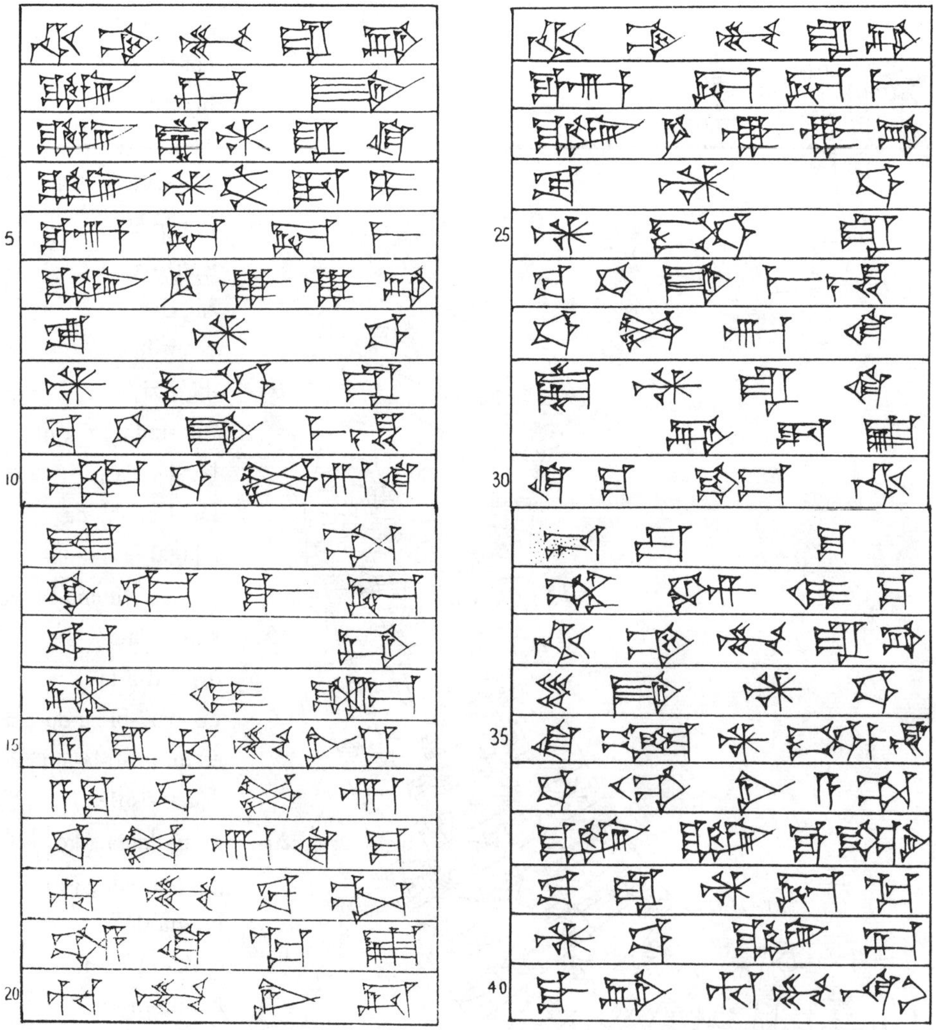

This is the Sumerian part of a bilingual text, and should be read in the light of the Akkadian original. See the List of Texts, p. XVII, 28.

29

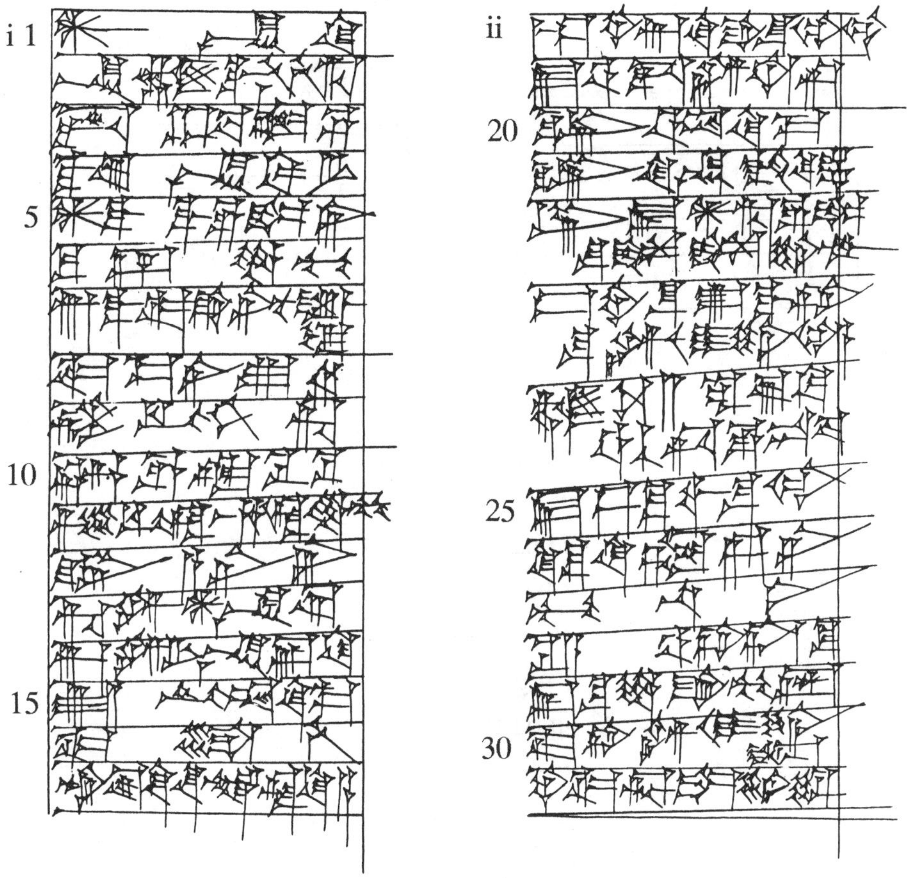

30

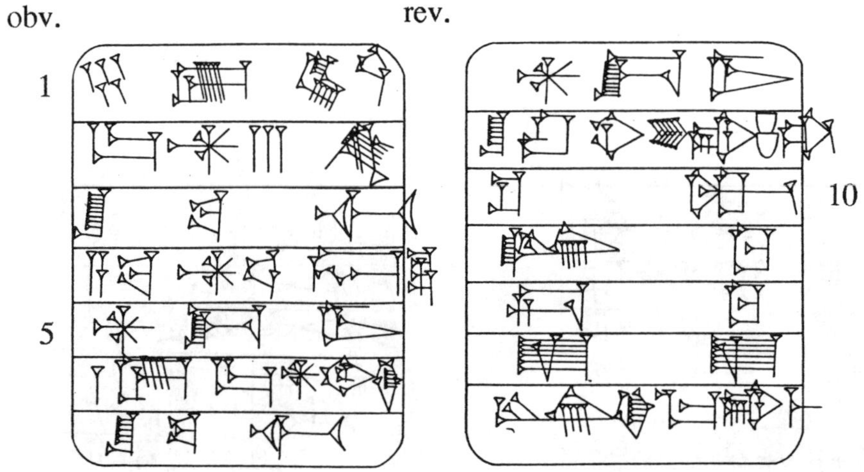

obv. 5 gig̃$_4$ kù-babbar
ur-^{d}eš$_5$-peš
šu ba-ti
a-ba-^{d}utu-gim-e
an-da-tuku
1 gig̃$_4$ ur-kèš^{ki}
šu ba-ti
rev. an-da-tuku
šu-rí-kam še-bi 0.2-ta
si-dam
lugal-DUR$_2$
gala
IŠ kuš$_7$
lú-ki-‹inim-›ma-bi-me

31

obv.

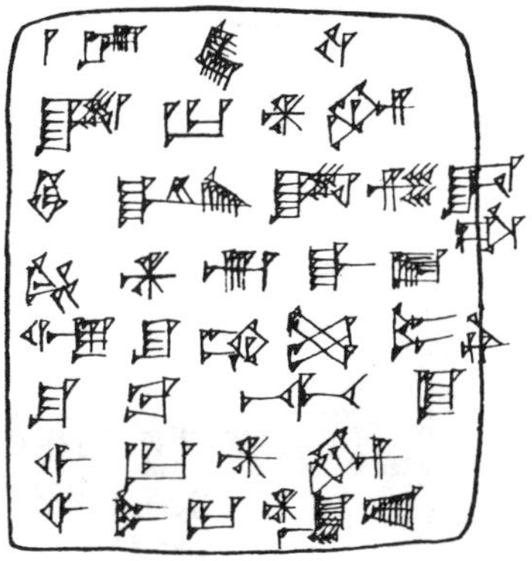

rev.

obv. 1 gig̃$_4$ kù-babbar
á-ur-^{d}iškur
ki-lugal-á-zi-da-ta
géme-^{d}nun-gal-ke$_4$
ù *šu-duran*(DUR$^{!}$.KIB) dumu-ni
šu ba-ti-éš
igi-ur-^{d}iškur
igi-dumu-ur-^{d}*sîn*
rev. igi-lú-^{d}iškur
igi-pú-ta dumu-lugal-ḫ̮é-g̃ál
tukum-bi
g̃á-la ba-dag
še 6 sìla-ta-a ág̃-dam
mu-lugal-bi in-pà
iti še-gur$_{10}$-ku$_5$
mu má-gur$_8$-maḫ̮-
^{d}en-líl-lá ba-ab-du$_8$

32

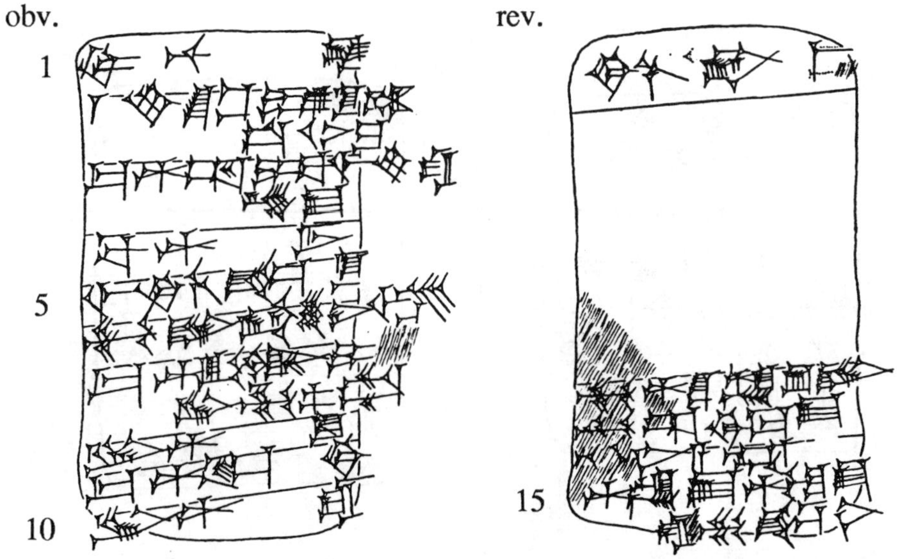

obv. di-til-la
^{I}šà-šu-níĝin dumu-ú-šè-ẖé-DU utul
ur-^{d}nanše dumu-ba-ši-šà-ra-gi-ke$_4$
ba-an-tuku
igi-di-ku$_5$-ne-šè
mu-lugal-bi in-pà-eš
ur-^{d}ig-alim dumu-lú-ĝu$_{10}$ maškim
lú-^{d}šára
ur-^{d}ištaran
lú-diĝir-ra
rev. di-ku$_5$-bi-me
(space)
mu ^{d}*šu*-^{d}*sîn* lugal-
uri$_5$^{ki}-ma-ke$_4$
na-rú-a-maẖ
^{d}en-líl ^{d}nin-líl-ra mu-ne-dù

33

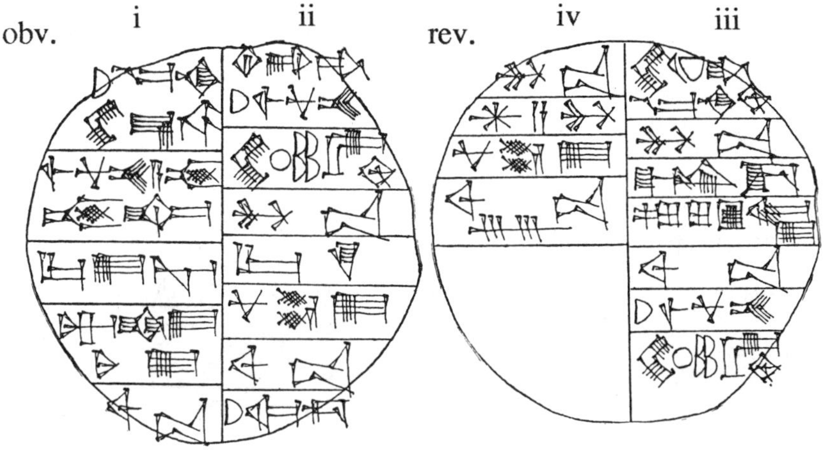

34

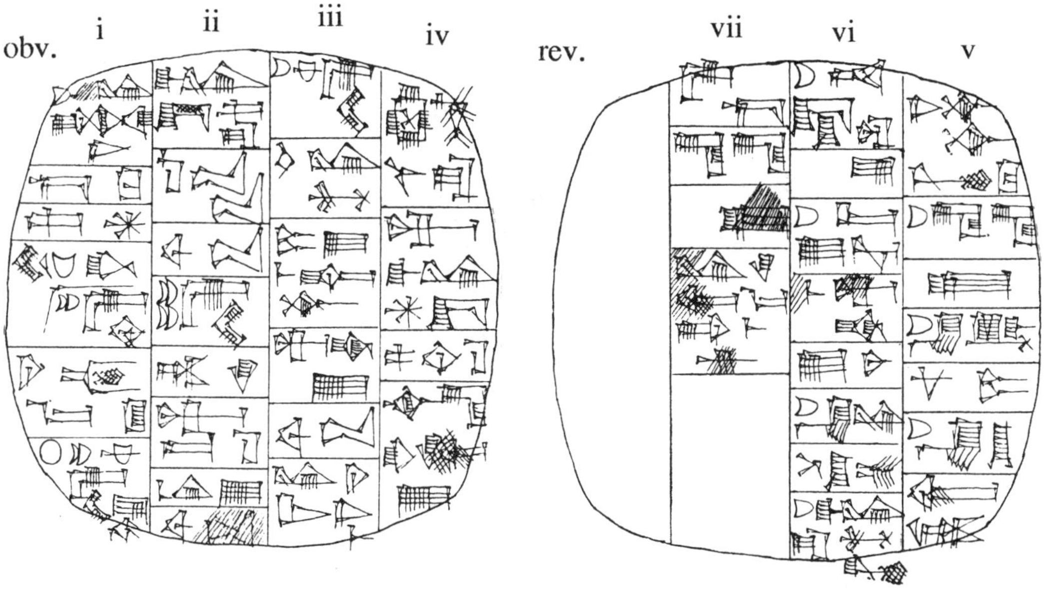

35

obv.

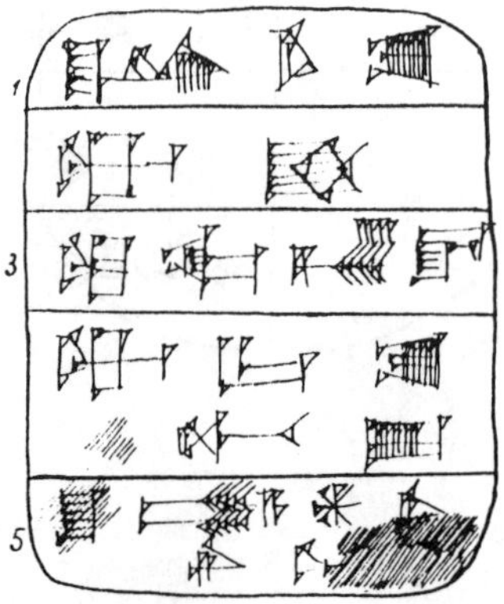

rev.

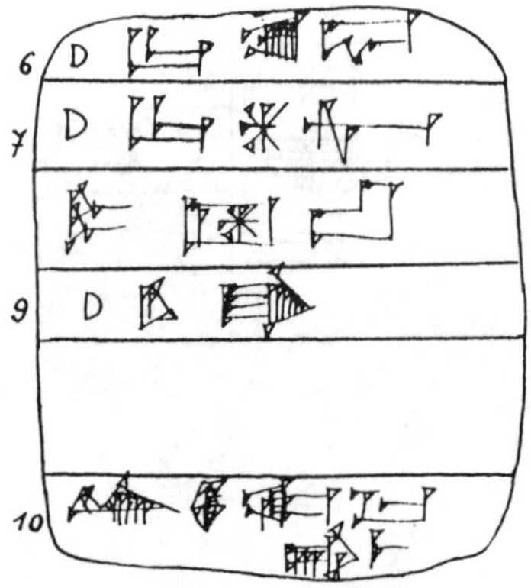

obv. 1 lugal-níĝ-zu
dam-gàr
nin-inim-zi-da
dam-ur-su nagar-ke$_4$
5 šu-du$_8$-a-an-ni ì-⸢DU⸣
rev. 6 ^{I}ur-su$^{!}$ šitim
^{I}ur-^{d}inanna
dumu-ama-iri
^{I}níĝ-gur$_{11}$
(space)
10 lú-ki-inim-ma-bi-me

36

obv.

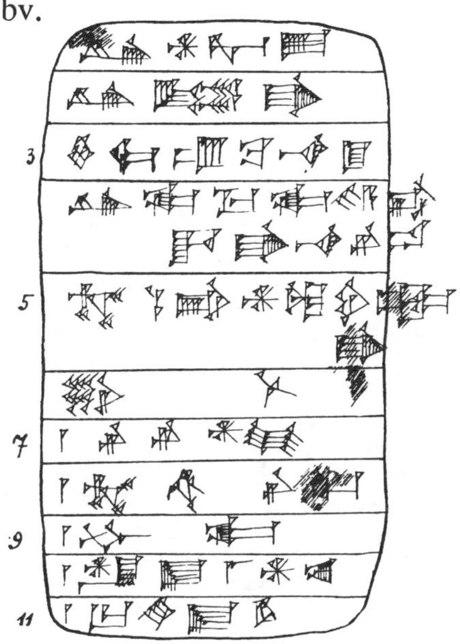

rev.

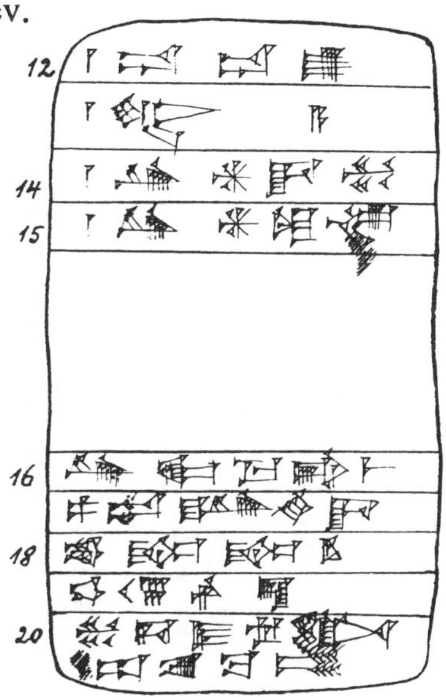

37

obv.

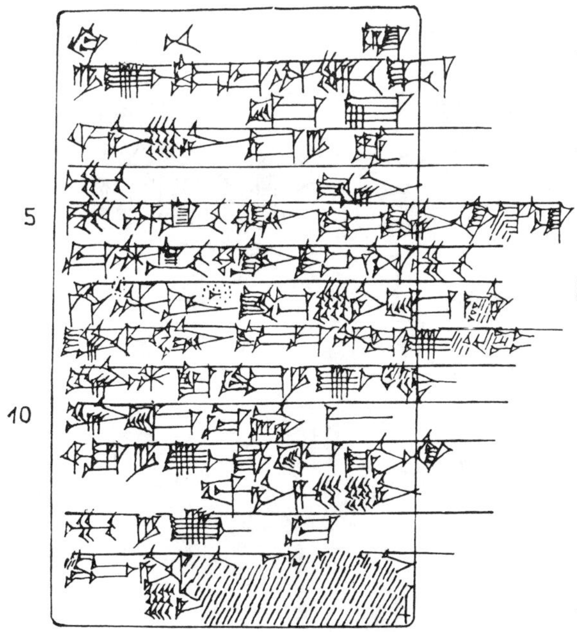

rev.

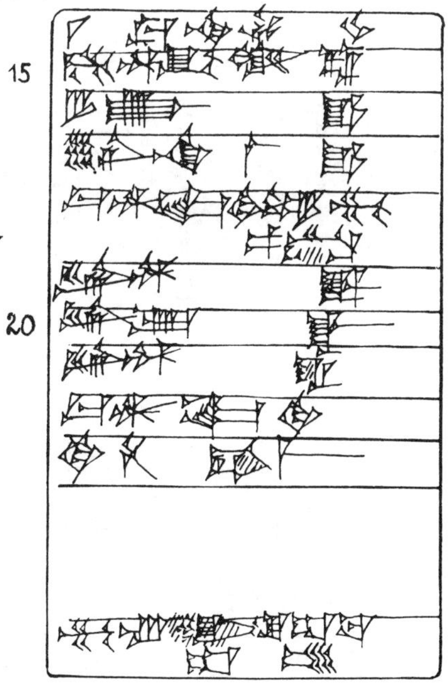

38

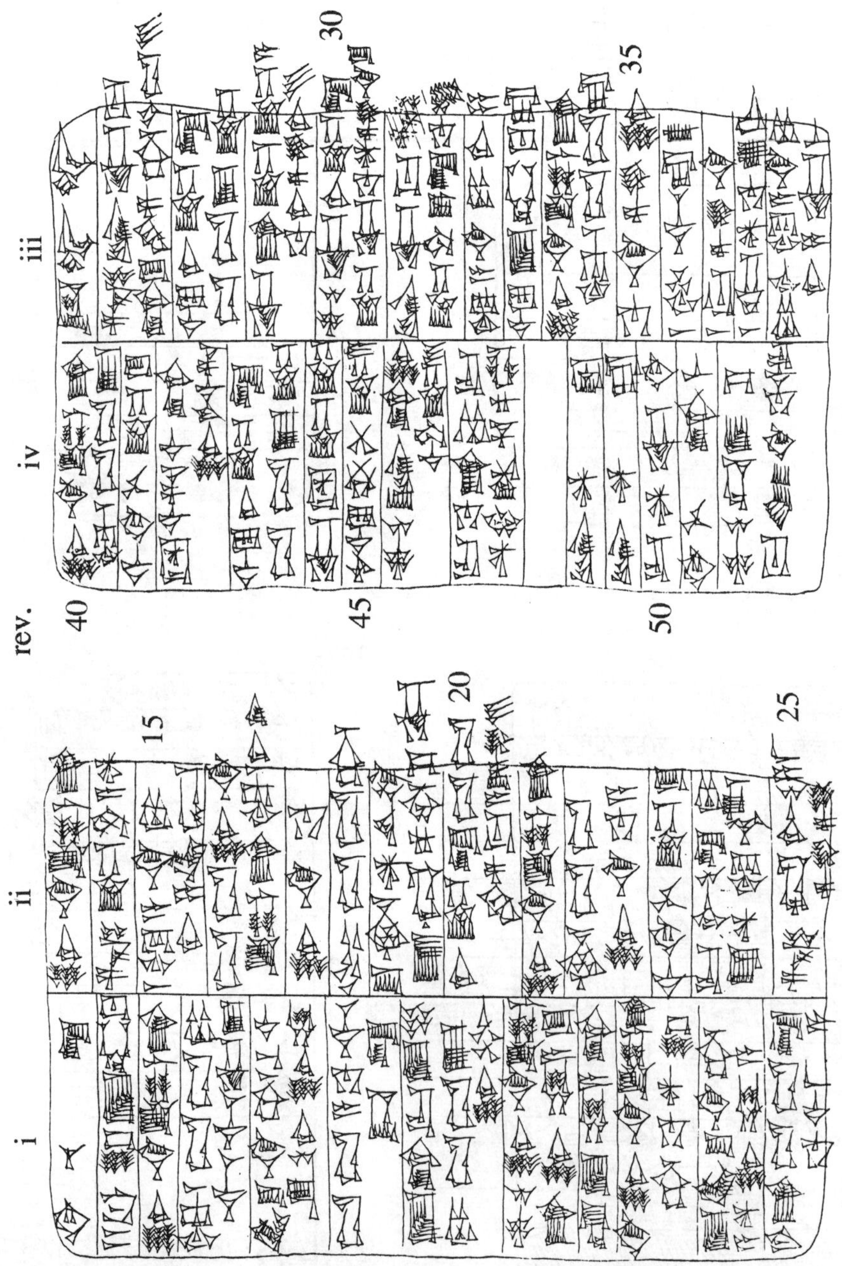

39

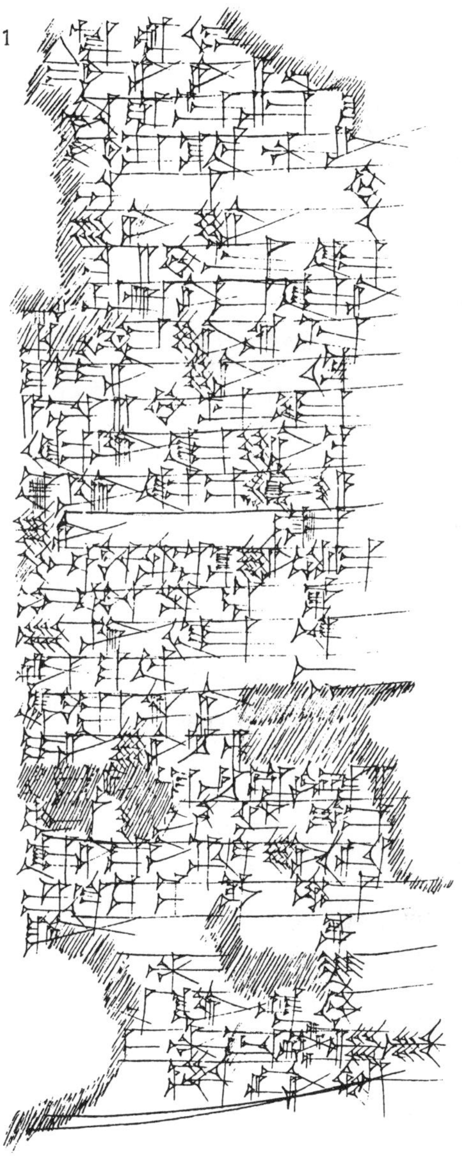

[^{d}]⸢*eštar*⸣-*um-m[i]*
[du]mu-mí-ì-lí-A.Z[U]
[^{d}]*èr-ra-ma-lik*-⸢e⸣
[na]m-dam-šè ba-an-tuku
[a-r]á-diš-kam
[es]ag̃$_{x}$ ([E$_{2}$].ŠE)-ni in-bùru
[a-r]á-min-kam-ma-ka
⸢^{dug}⸣šab-ì-g̃iš-ka-ni
⸢g̃ál⸣ bí-in-taka$_{4}$-*ma*
túg i-ni-in-dul
a-rá-eš$_{5}$-kam-ma-ka
ugu-lú-ka in-dab$_{5}$
su-lú-ka g̃iš-nú-a
in-kéš
pu-úḫ-ru-um-šè in-íl
pu-úḫ-ru-um-e
mu lú ugu-na
al-dab$_{5}$-ba-aš
kù-dam-taka$_{4}$-ni [x] m[a-na kù-babbar]
i-ni-in-g̃ar-r[e-eš]
⸢kiši$_{4}$$^{?}$ x ù⸣ sur-ra gal$_{4}$-la-⸢a⸣-[ni]
⸢umbin in⸣-ku$_{5}$-ru-ne
giri$_{17}$-ni $^{g̃iš}$gag-si-sá in-bùru-uš
iri^{ki} NIG̃IN$_{2}$.NIG̃IN$_{2}$-e-dè
lugal-e
[ba]-an-sè
[di-dab$_{5}$-b]a-lugal-la-kam
[^{d}*iš-m*]*e*-^{d}*da-gan*-zi-g̃u$_{10}$
maškim-bi-im

The interpretation of the faint traces at the beginning of line 21 as kiši$_{4}$ is highly tentative, though persuasive. Accordingly, the sign kiši$_{4}$ has not been included in the Sign List, and the reader is referred to the information given on p. XVII, 39.

40

i ii

obv.

1 1

5

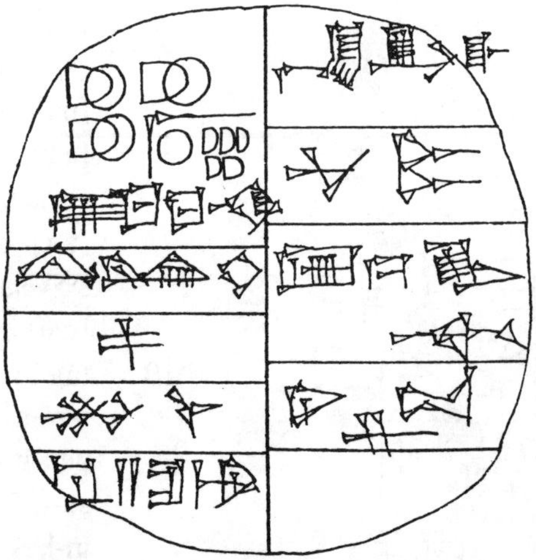

reverse blank

obv. i	1	1800 lá 15 sa ‹ú-›durun$_x$-na
		šeš-lú-du$_{10}$
		ugula
		mu-ku$_5$
	5	má-2 e-me-g̃ar
obv. ii	1	en-ig-gal
		nu-bànda
		g̃anun-g̃iš-kíg̃-ti
		ì-DU 2

41

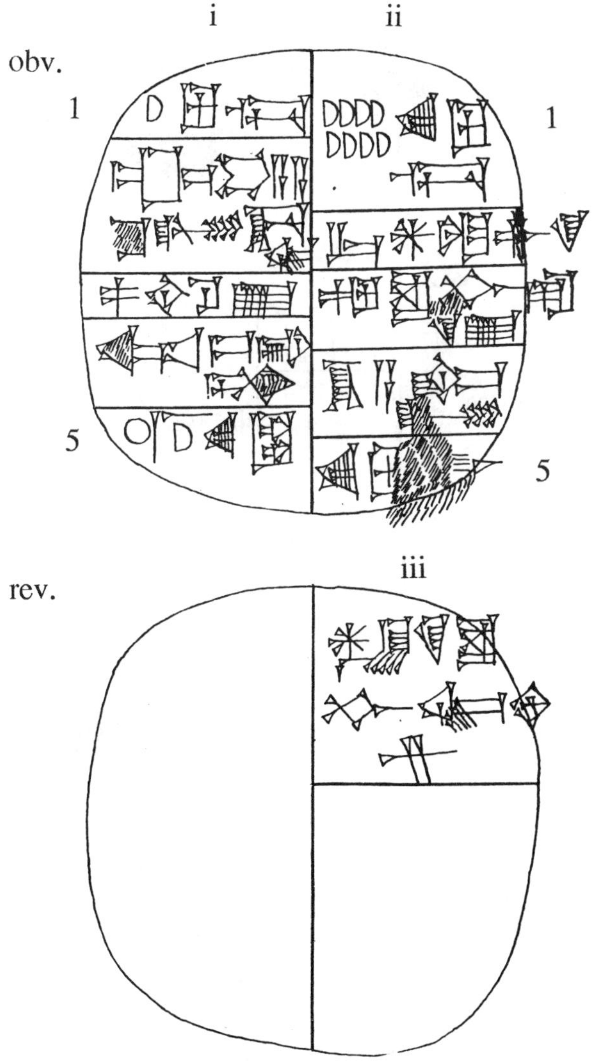

(i 1) 1 udu-nita / ezem-amar-a-a-⸢si⸣-ge$_4$-da-ka / énsi-ke$_4$ / ⸢abzu⸣ g̃iš bi-tag / *(5)* 10 lá 1 kuš-u$_8$ /
(ii 1) 8 kuš-udu-nita / ur-^{d}nin-mar^{ki} / sipa-pa$_5$-sír-ra^{ki}-ke$_4$ / šu-a bí-gi$_4$ / *(5)* kuš-ud[u] ⸢ú⸣-rum- /
(iii 1) ^{d}en-ki-pa$_5$-sír-ka-kam 2

42

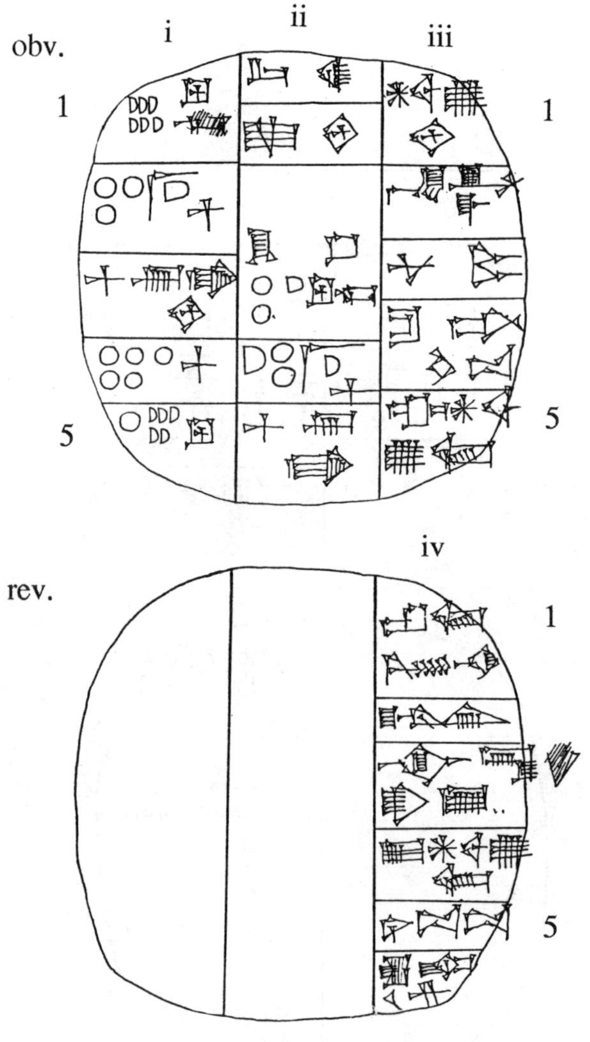

(i 1) 6 udu-⸢nita⸣ / 30 lá 1 maš / maš-aša$_5$-ga-kam / 50 maš / *(5)* 15 udu /

(ii 1) ur-du$_6$ / kuš$_7$-kam / šu-nígin 21 udu-nita / 80 lá 1 maš / *(5)* maš-aša$_5$-ga- /

(iii 1) ^{d}ba-U$_2$-kam / en-ig-gal / nu-bànda / e-ta-è / *(5)* ezem-^{d}ba-U$_2$-ka

(iv 1) iri-KA-gi-na / lugal- / lagaš$^{\ulcorner ki \urcorner}$-ke$_4$ / é-^{d}ba-U$_2$-ka / *(5)* ì-laḫ$_5$ / zà bí-šuš 2

43

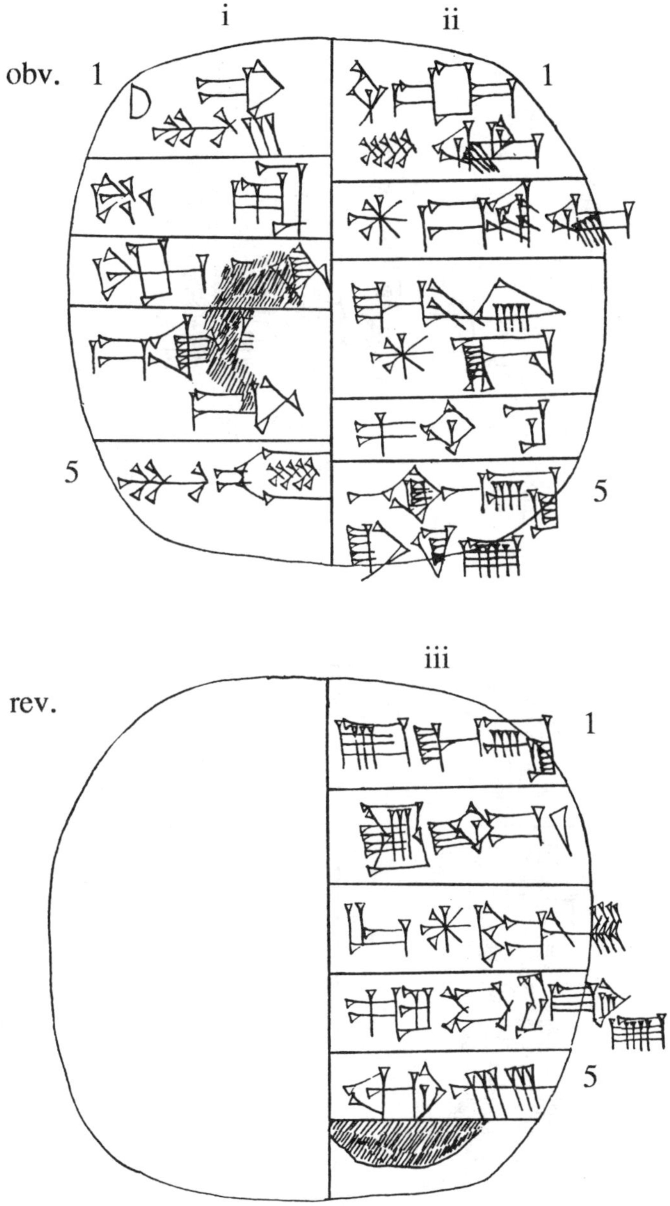

44

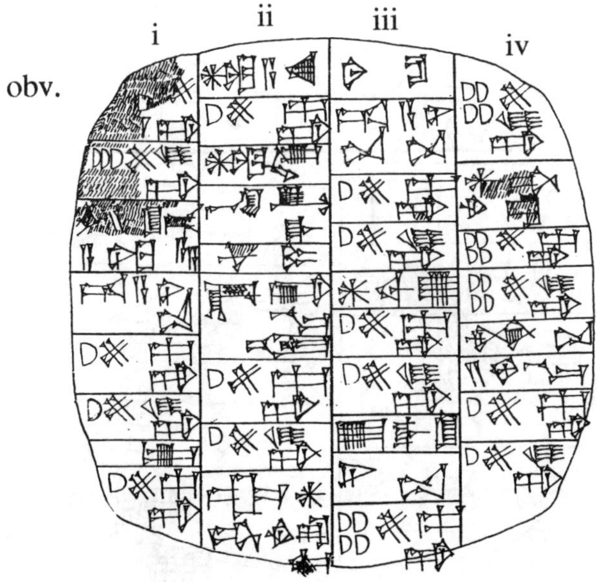

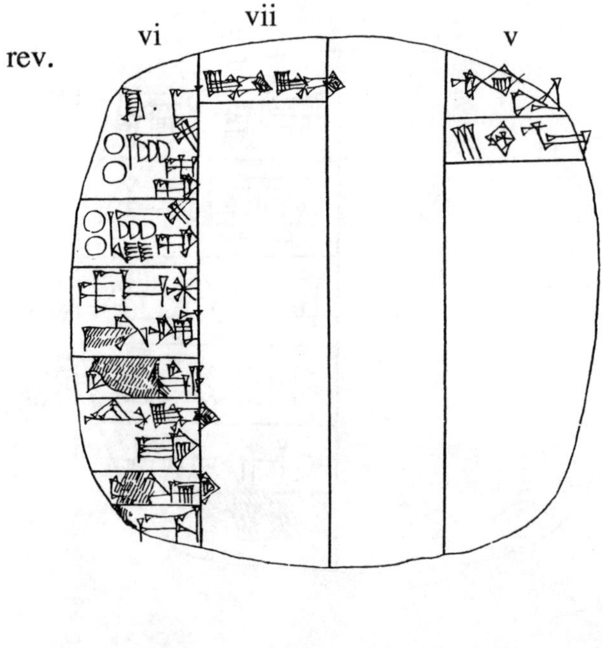

SIGN LIST

This list is limited to the signs that occur in the texts in this book and arranges them, in the column on the right, according to their Neo-Assyrian order. It is to these numbers that the numbers in the alphabetically arranged List of Phonetic Values refer.

The second column to the right lists the values that the signs have in the texts in this book. The central column presents the signs in chronological order. It does not include every variant, since the same sign can be written somewhat differently within the same text. The forms are typical and are intended to help the reader in identifying the signs.

The column to the left, column **L**, refers to R. Labat, Manuel d'épigraphie akkadienne, Paris 1976[5]. Since the sign numbers in R. Labat, with minor exceptions, are the same as those in R. Borger, Assyrisch-babylonische Zeichenliste (ABZ), Kevelaer/Neukirchen-Vluyn 1978 (AOAT 33; Ergänzungsband AOAT 33A; 1981), the reader may use the **L**(abat) numbers to find the same signs in R. Borger, ABZ. Furthermore these numbers refer, again with minor exceptions, to A. Deimel's mostly outdated, but sometimes still useful book, Šumerisches Lexikon, II. Vollständige Ideogramm-Sammlung. 4 Vols. (Roma 1928-1933; reeditio photomechanica 1961).

In addition, chapter V "Zeichennamen" in R. Borger's Assyrisch-babylonische Zeichenliste (ABZ), 376-413 is highly recommended to the reader of this book as a reference list.

Labat = Borger	chronolog. geordnete Zeichen	Bedeut. d. Zeich. i. diesem Buch	neuass. Zeichen	Nr. d. Zeichen i. diesem Buch
L 1		rum		1
5		ba	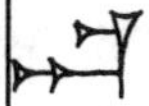	2
6		zu sú	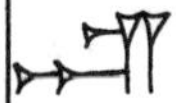	3
6		abzu	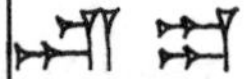	3a
7		su kuš		4
8	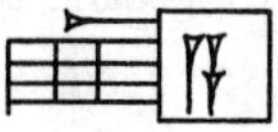	šen		5
9	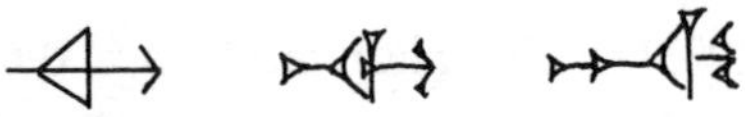	bal bala	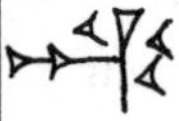	6
10	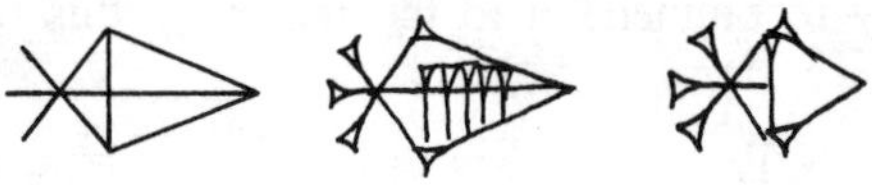	ğir		7
11	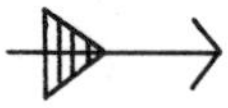	ušum		8
12	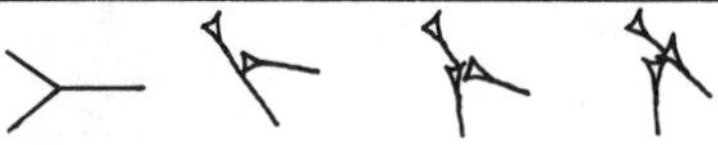	ku_5 sila tar		9
13		an diğir am_6		10

L 15	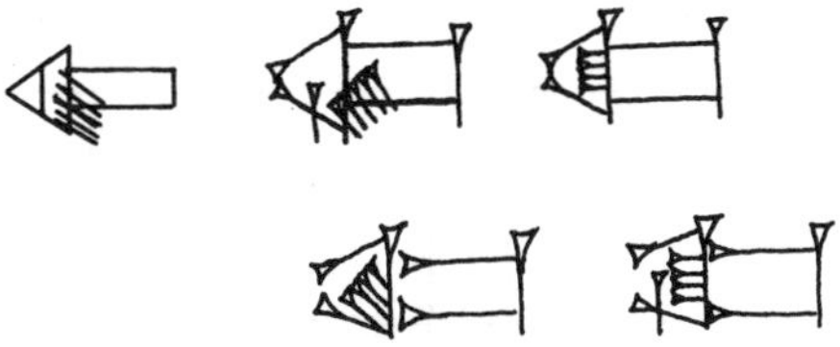	ka gù du_{11} inim zú $giri_{17}$		11
15		ištaran		11a
36		gu_7		12
38		uru iri rí		13
40		unken		14
43	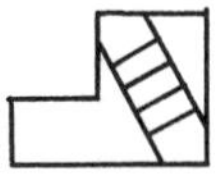	uru_x		15
46***	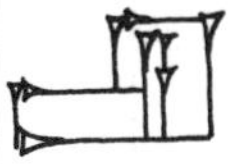	URUxA		16a
49*		ĝišgal u_{18}	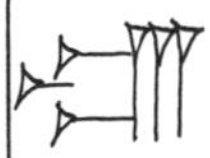	16b
50		èr	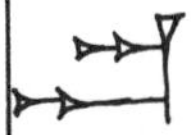	17

L				
50/51		úrdu	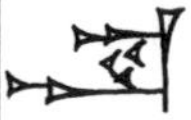	18
52		iti		19
53		šubur		20
55	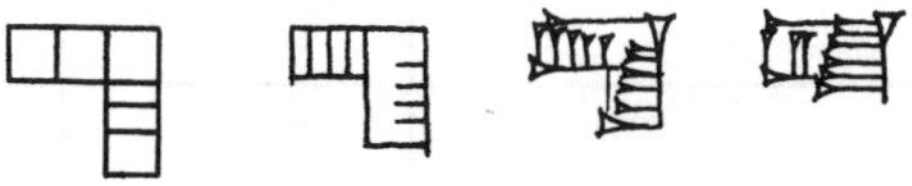	la	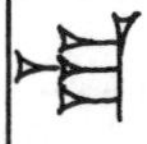	21
56	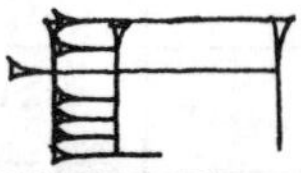	engar	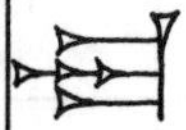	22
57	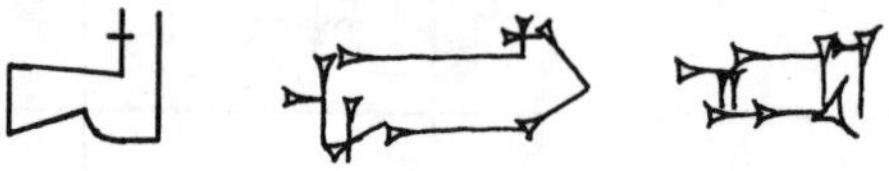	maḫ	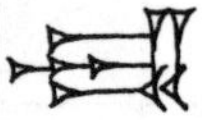	23
58	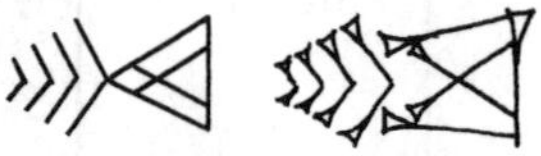  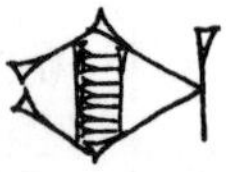	dú tu ku_4 gur_8	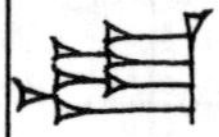	24
59	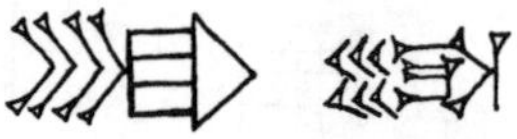	le li èn	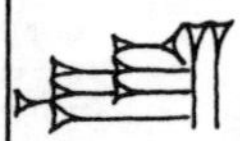	25
60		kúr		26

L			
60	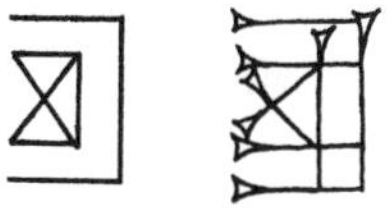	pa_5	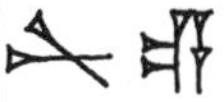 26a
61	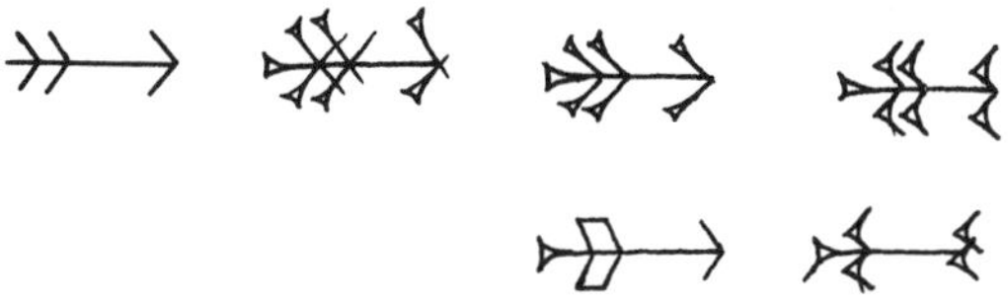	mu $\tilde{g}u_{10}$	 27
62		sìla	 28
62		sagi	 28a
63		$taka_4$	 29
67	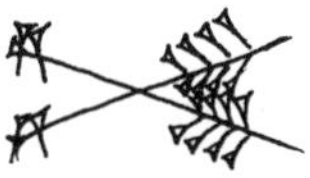	gi_{16}	 30
68	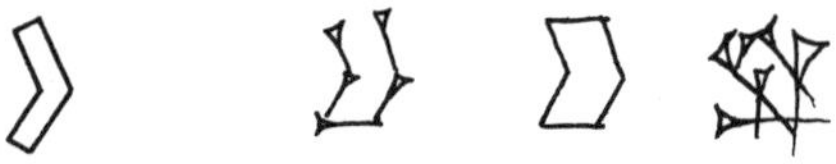	ru šub	 31
69		til	 32
70		na	 33
71		šir	 34
71		lagaš/s	 34a

L 72		numun	 35
73	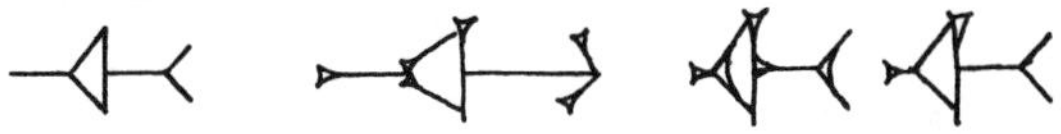	ti	 36
74	  	bar maš $\frac{1}{2}$	 37
75		nu	 38
76		máš	 39
78		ḫu mušen	 40
79	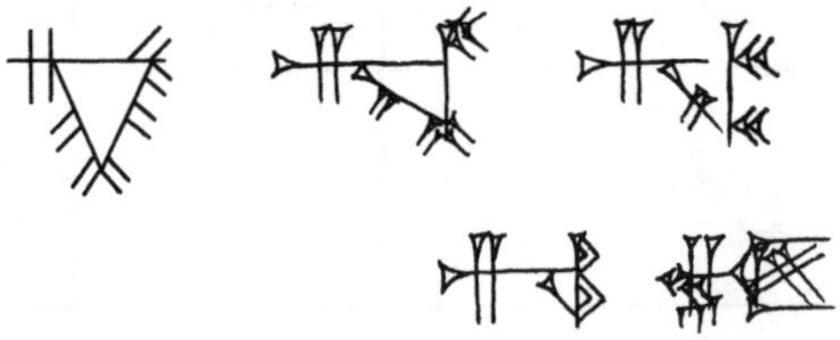	nam	 41
80	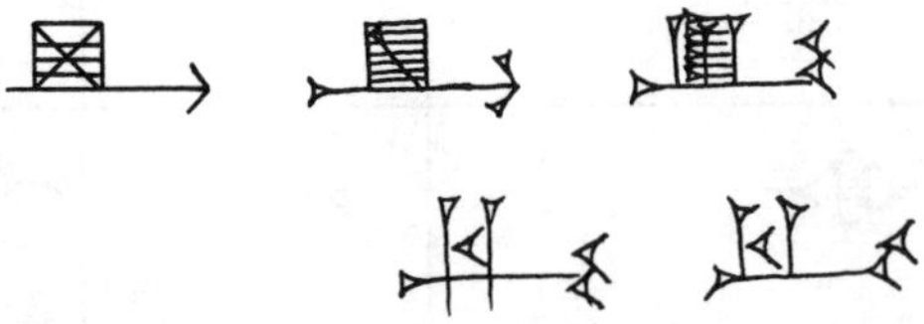	ig g̃ál	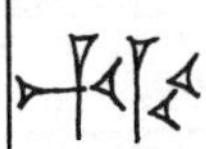 42

L			
82		sa_4	 43
84	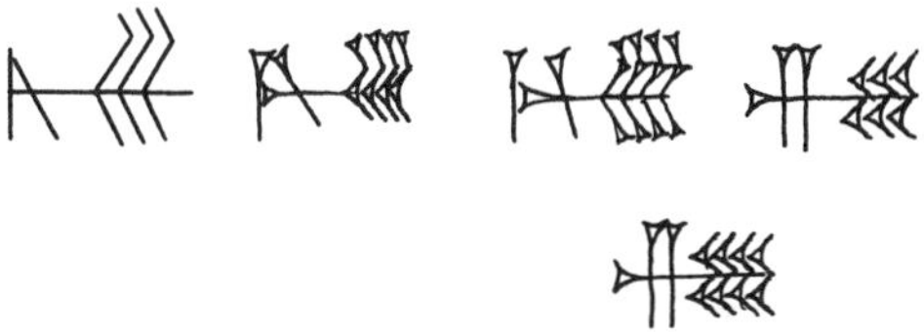	zi	 44
ABZ 66C	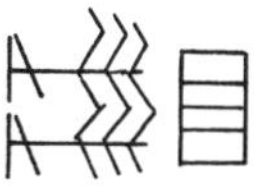	$\check{s}ub_5$	44a
85	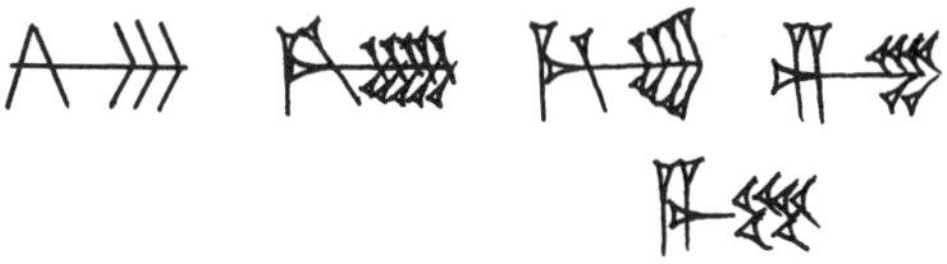	ge gi sig_{17}	 45
86		re ri	 46
87	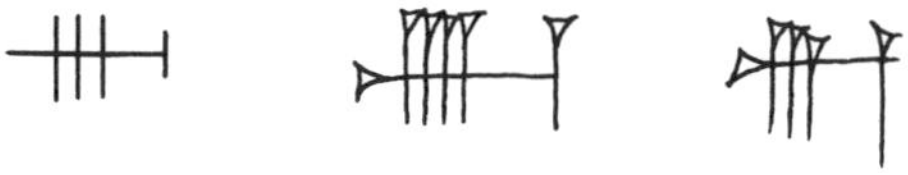	nun	 47
87		eridu	 47a
90		gada	 48
92		akkil	 49

L			
92b		umbin	 50
95	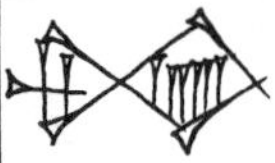	mun	 51
97	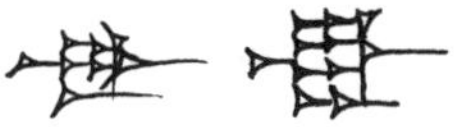	ak(a)	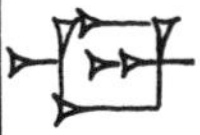 52
99	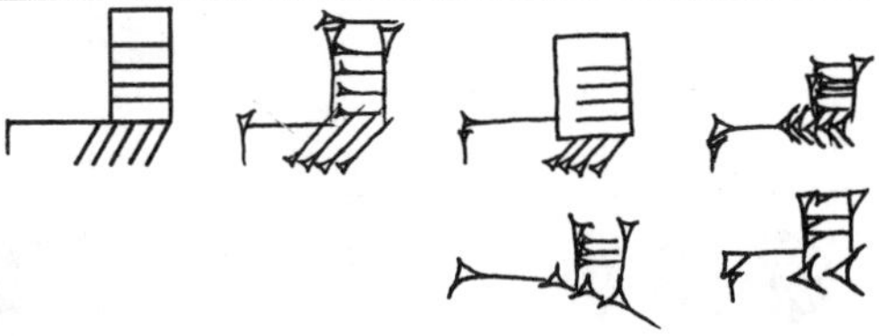	en uru_{16} su'en sîn	 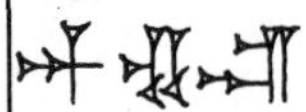 53a
100	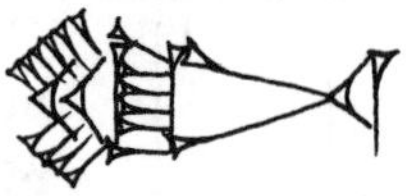	dàra	 54
101		sur šur	 55
103		mùš	 56
103		inanna	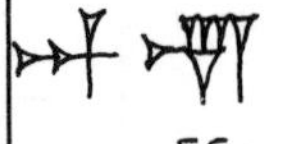 56a
103c		šùba	 56b
104		sa ašgab	 57  57a

L			
105		gána asa$_5$ kár	 58
106		gú	 59
108	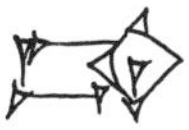	dur	 60
ABZ 108		duran	 60a
111		gur	 61
112		si	 62
114		dar	 63
115		sag̃	 64
122		má	 65
122b	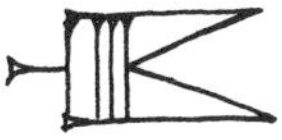	ud$_5$	 66
123		diri	 67

L			
124		límmu	 68
126		tag	 69
128		ab èš	 70
129a	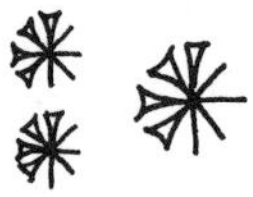	mul	 71
133	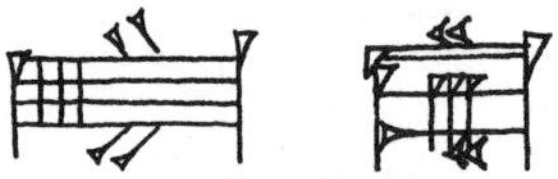	ká	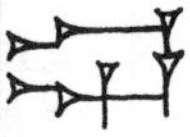 72
134		um	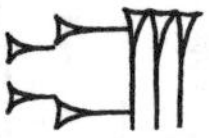 73
138		dub	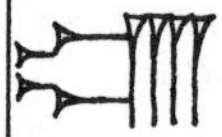 74
139	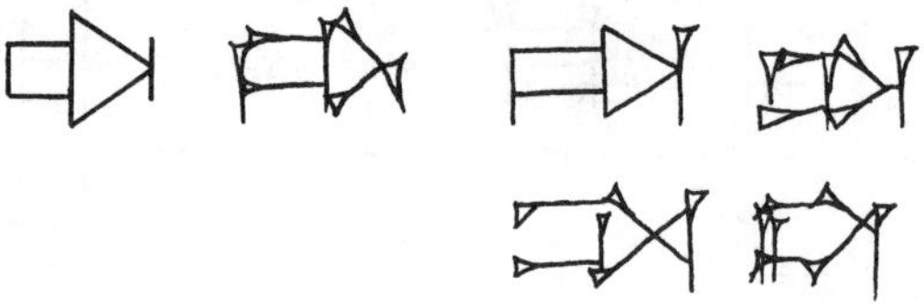	ta	 75
142	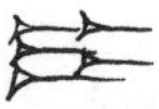	i	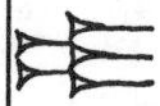 76
143	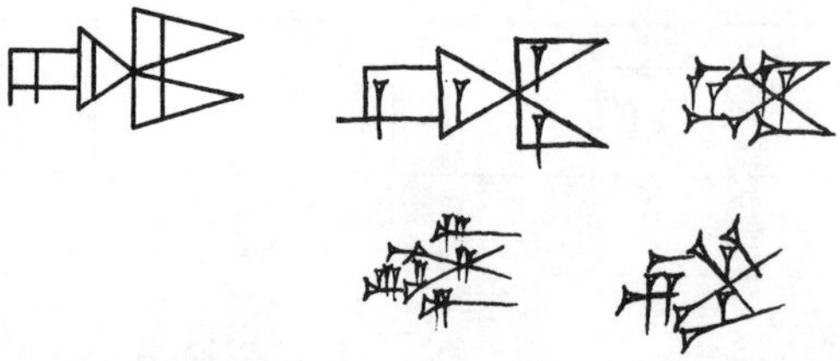	gan ḫé	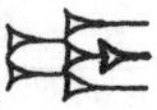 77

L			
144		bànda dumu	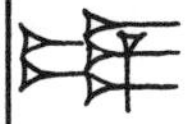 78
144		íbila	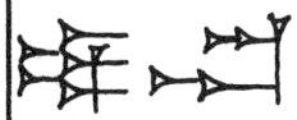 78a
145	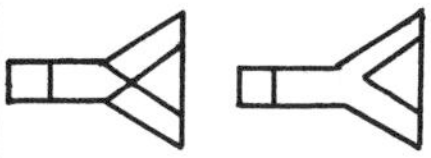	ad	 79
148	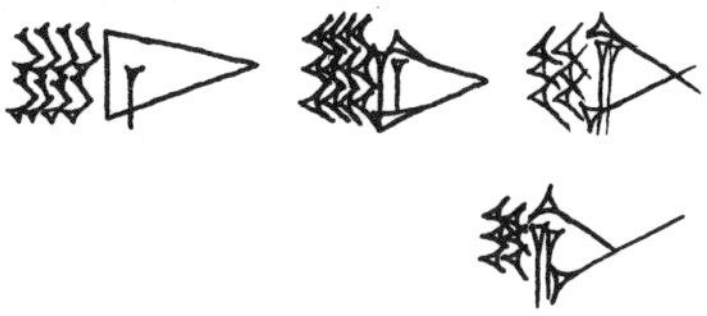	in	 80
151	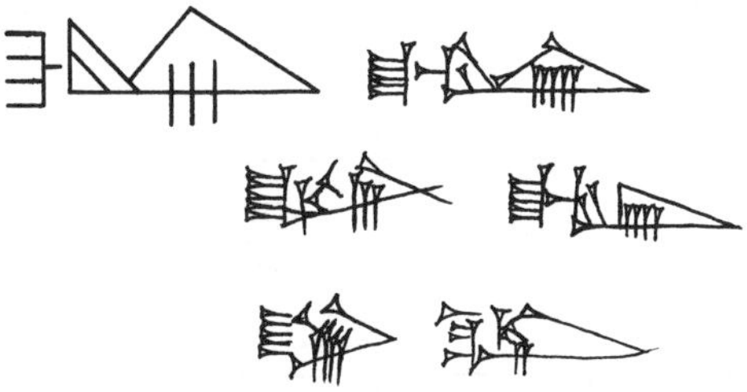	lugal	 81
152	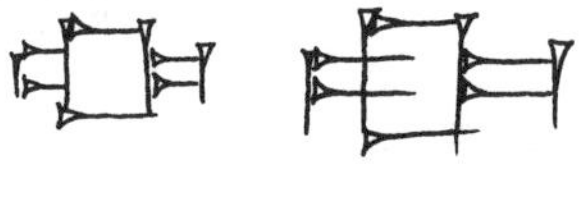	ezem/n	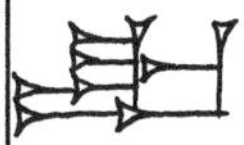 82
		$asila_x$	EZENxŠID 83
152[8]	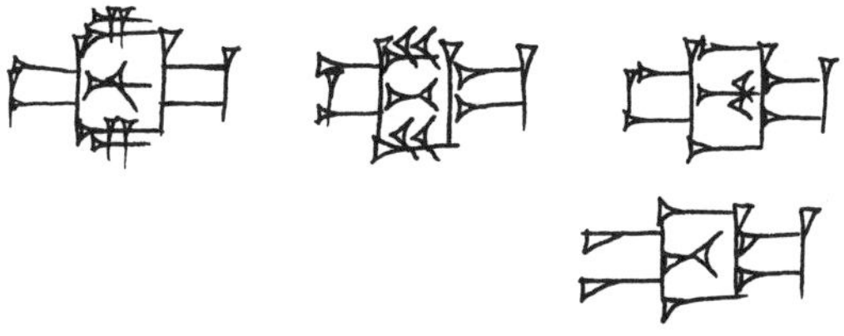	bàd $u\tilde{g}_5$	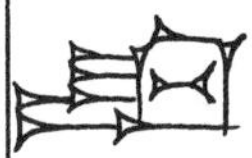 84

L				
152	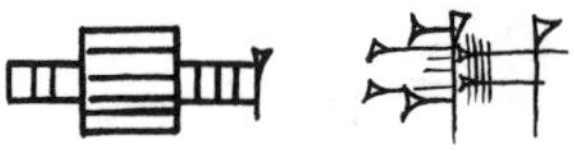	késˇ	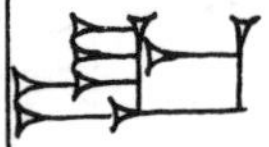	85
152	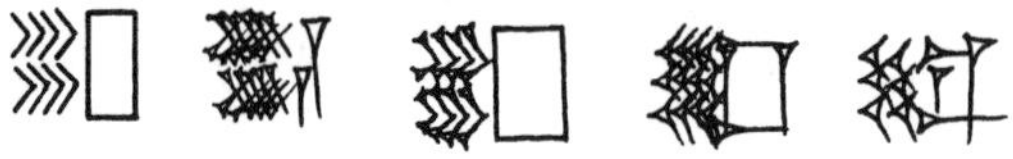	mú sar	[1] 	86
164		sè šúm		87
166		kas		88
167	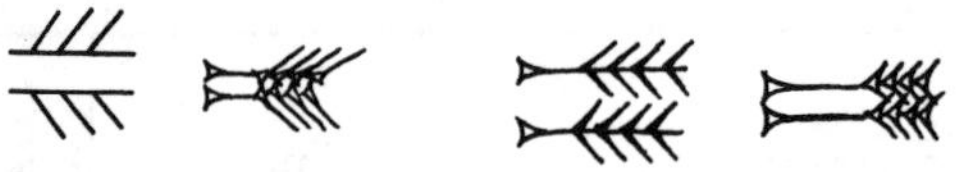	du_8		89
168	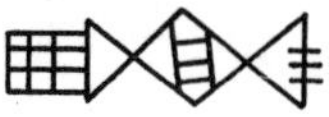	eden		90
170		am	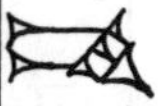	91
172	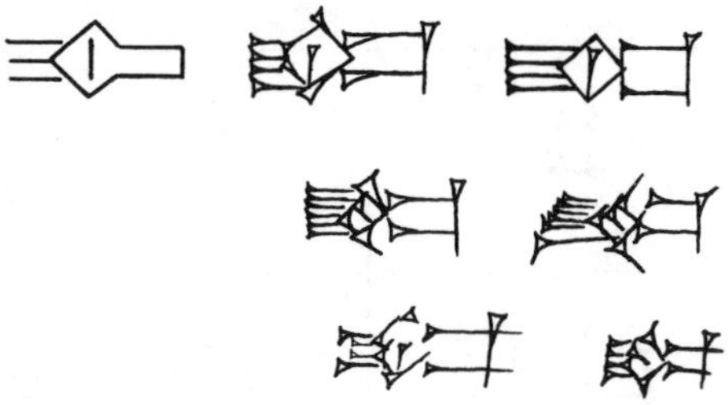	bí dè izi li_9 ne		92
172		érim		92a

[1] The position of this sign according to Neo-Assyrian order follows R. Labat, Manuel d'épigraphie akkadienne, Paris 1976[5], 104-105, although this sign should be placed among the signs that begin with three horizontals. This inconsistency is due to the ancient scribes outside of Niniveh, who sometimes wrote this sign with only two horizontals, as if SAR and $KEŠ_2$ were the same sign in Neo-Assyrian script. See R. Borger, ABZ, 138, sign 331e ("Auch wie n 152").

L			
173		gibil	 93
183	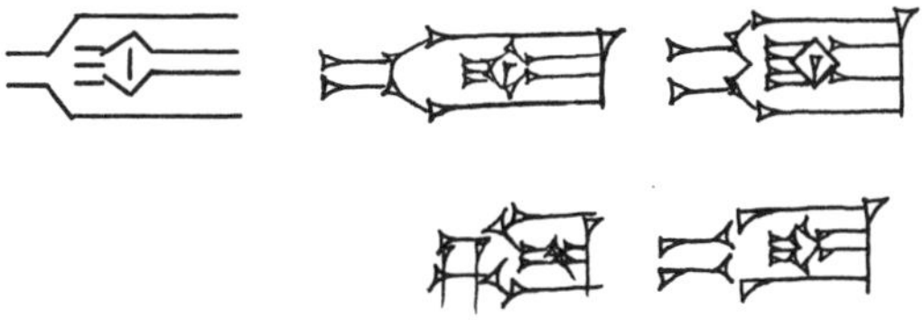	áğ	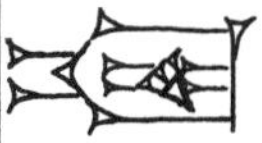 94
187		sa_{10} sám	 95
191	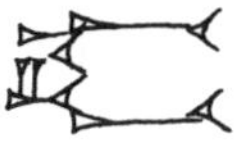	gum	 96
195		$gunu_4$	 97
195		unug	 97a
200		nanše	 98
200		nina	 98a
201	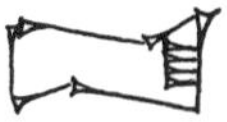	suḫuš	 99
202	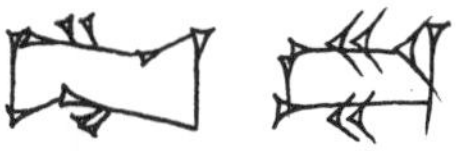	kas_4	 100

L 206 ABZ 206	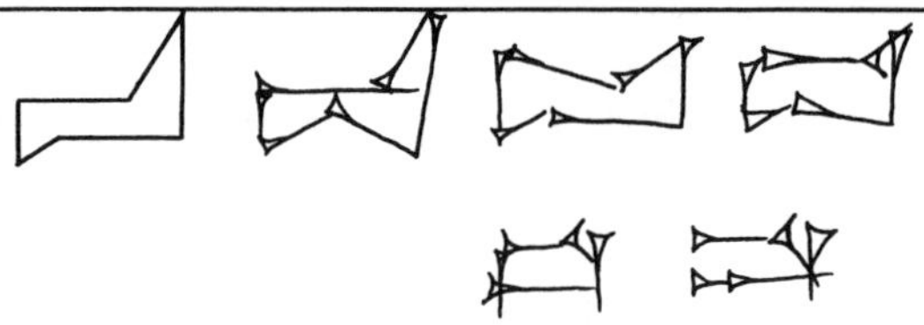	gub g̃en du de$_6$ túm rá re$_6$ laḫ$_5$	 101 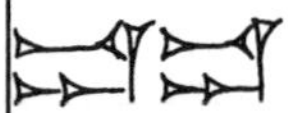 101a
207		íb	 102
208 208	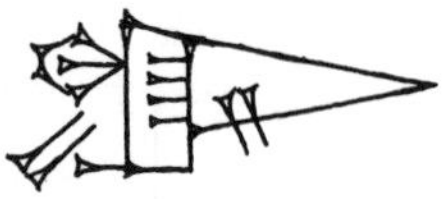	anše dùr	 103 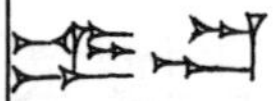 103a
210	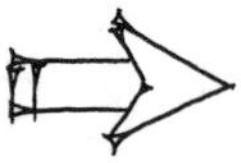	g̃eštin	 104
211 211	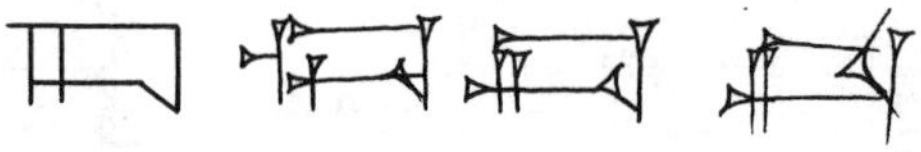	ús uš nita gala	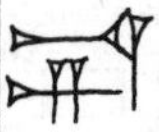 105  105a
212		iš kuš$_7$ saḫar	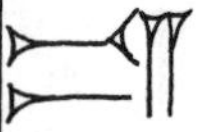 106
214	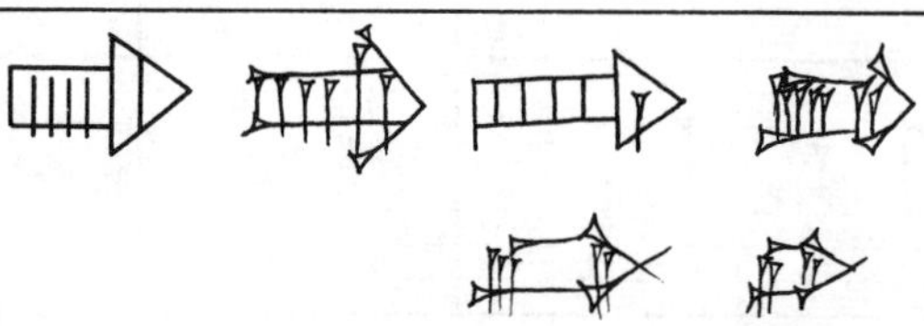	bé bi	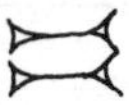 107

L				
214c		bàppir		107a
215	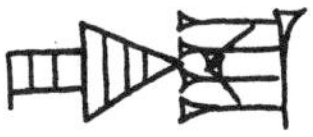	šim	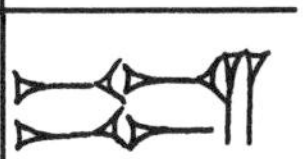	108
228		kib		109
229		na_4	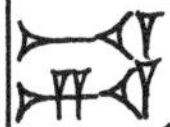	110
230		gag dù rú		111
231	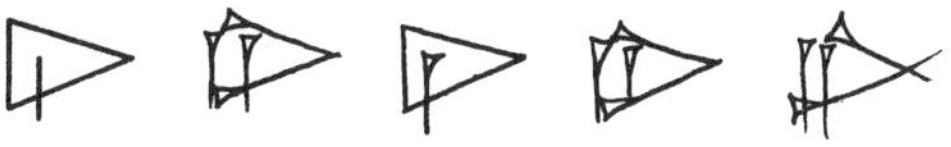	zal î lí né ni		112
231		dilmun		112a
232		ir		113
233	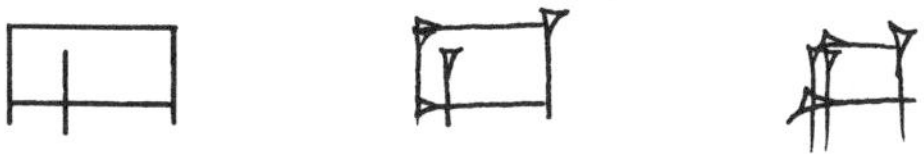	ğá $ğe_{26}$		114
233	ABZ 233,22 	šita		114a
237	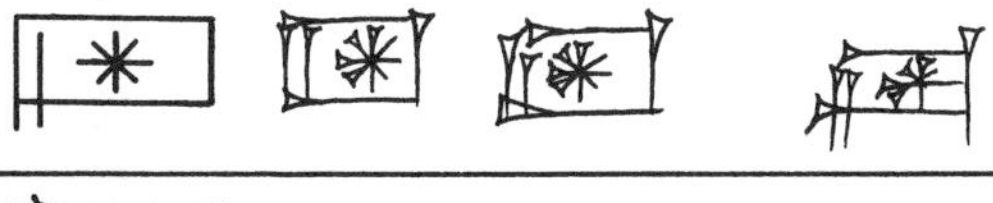	ama dağal	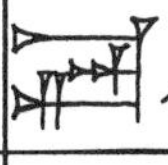	115
244	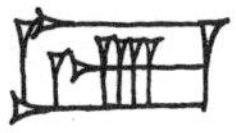	ğanun	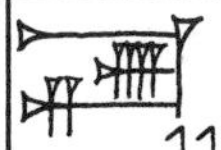	116

L			
249		kisal par$_4$	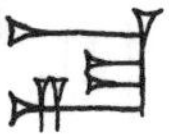 117
252	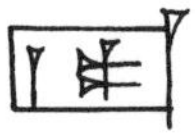	sila$_4$	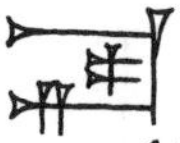 118
255	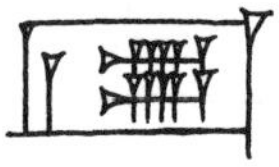	ùr uru$_{12}$	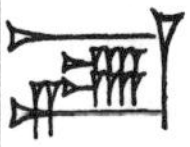 119
278	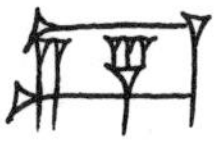	g̃alga	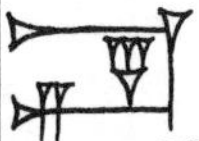 120
280	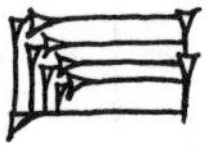	dag	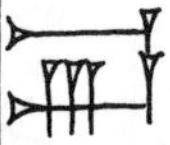 121
295	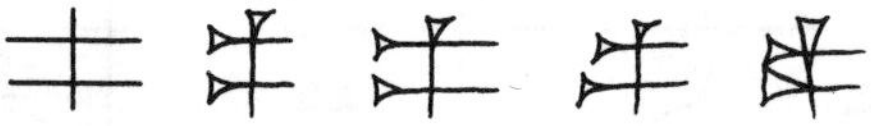	pa g̃idru ugula	 122
295c		rig$_7$	 122a
295d		maškim	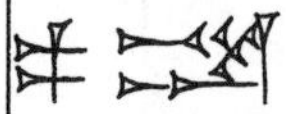 122b
295k		šab	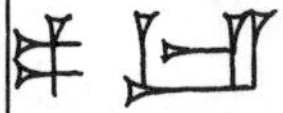 122c
295		énsi	 122d
295m		sipa	 122e
296		g̃iš	 123
152	ABZ 331e	kiri$_6$	 123a
296		g̃éštu	 123b
296		g̃èštu	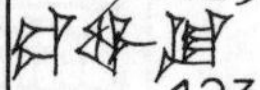 123c

L			
297		gu$_4$	 124
298		al	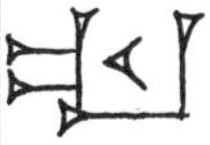 125
306		ub	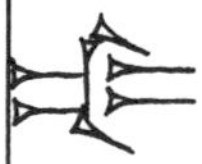 126
307		mar	 127
308	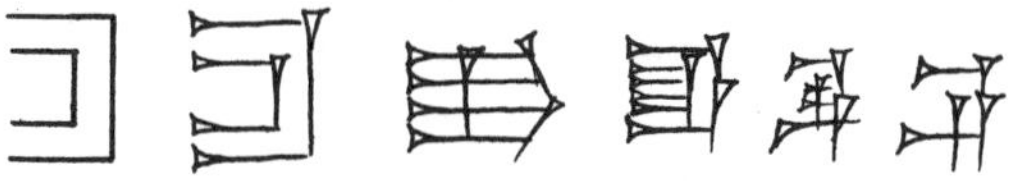	e	 128
309	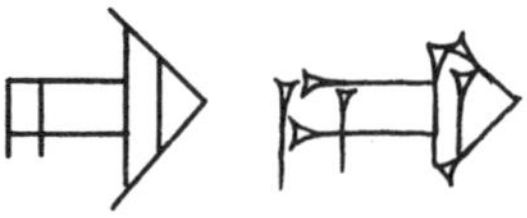	dug	 129
309		báḫar	 129a
312	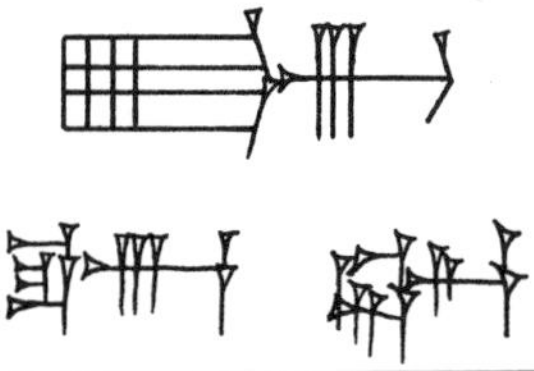	ùğ un kalam	 130
313	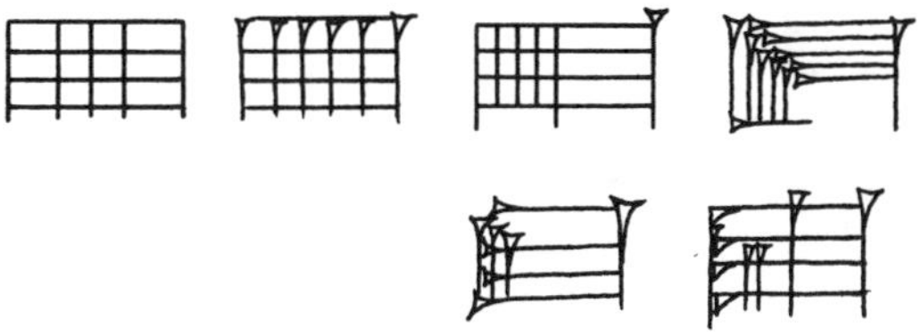	ke$_4$ líl	 131
314		sağğa	 132

L			
318		ú	 133
319 319	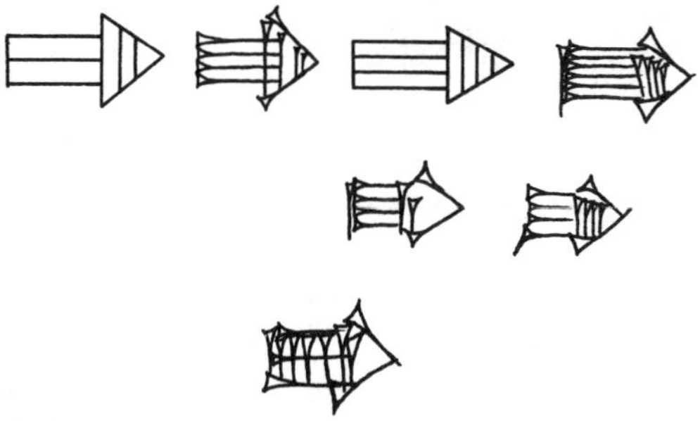	ga gur_{11} gára	 134  134a
320	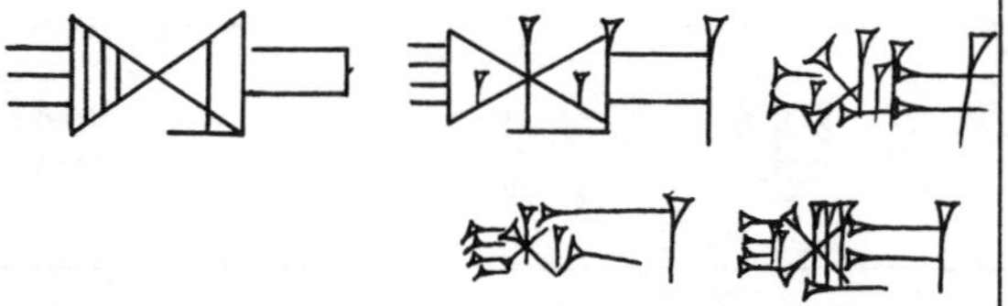	gùr íl	 135
321		luḫ sukkal	 136
322 322	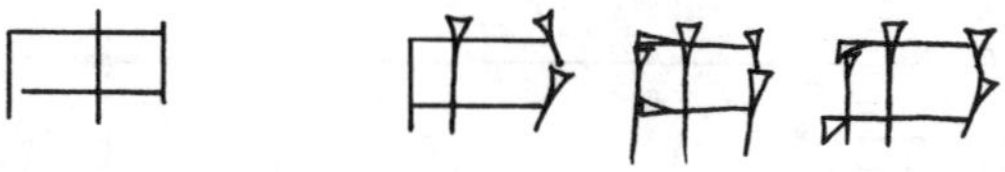	ĝuruš kala sig_{15} esi	 137 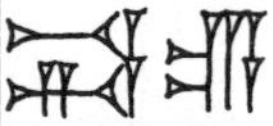 137a
324	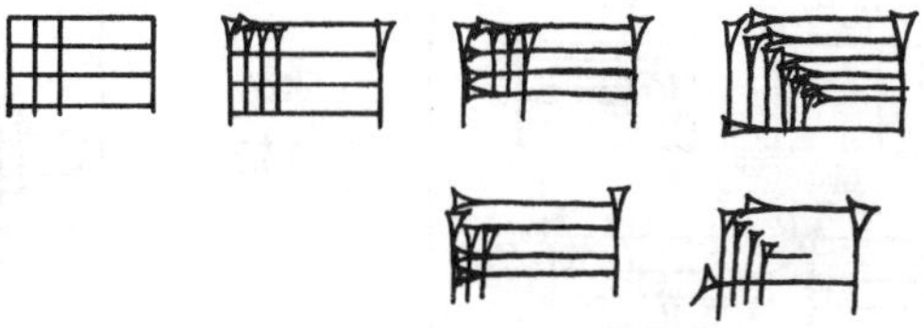	é $esa\tilde{g}_x$	 138  138a

L			
325		nir	 139
326		gi_4 ge_4	 140
328	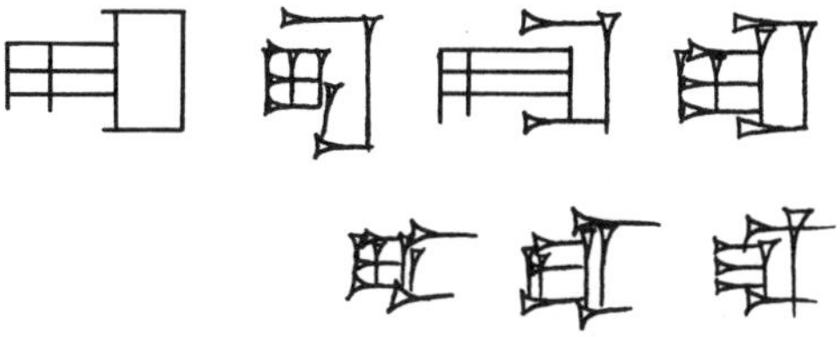	ra	 141
330	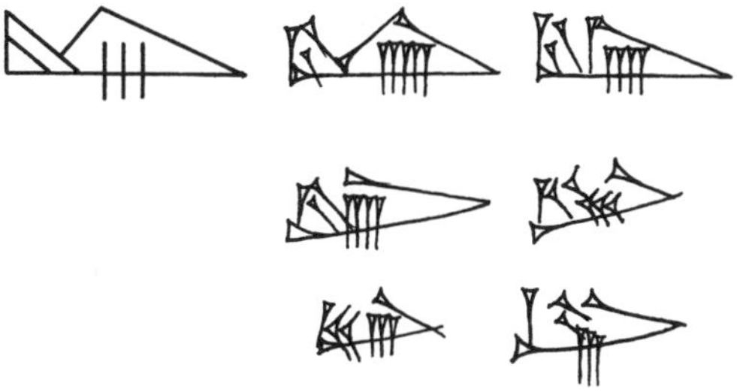	lú	 142
331	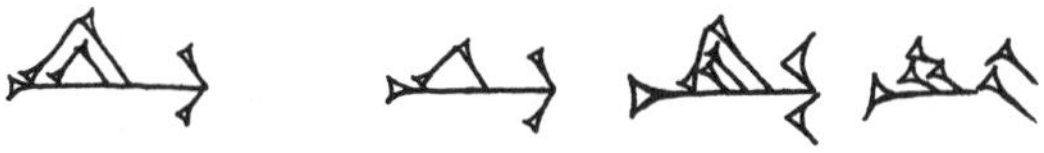	urin šeš	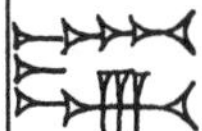 143
331		úri	 143a
331		uri_5	 143b
331		nanna	 143c
322		zà	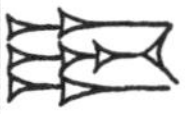 144

L			
333	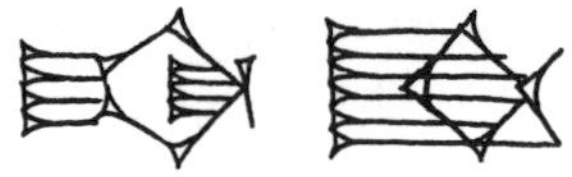	gàr	 145
334	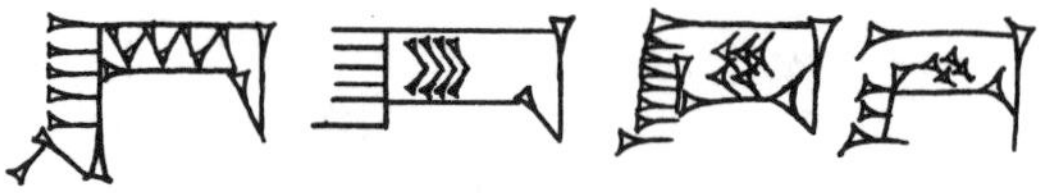	á	 146
335	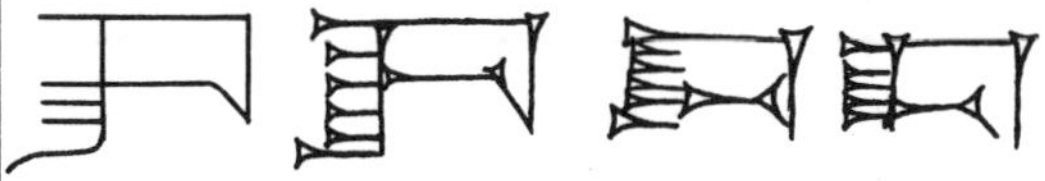	da	 147
338	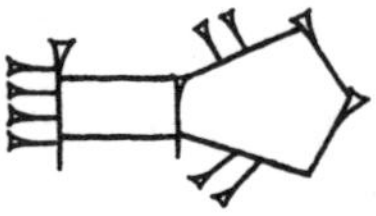	dé	 148
339		áš	 149
342	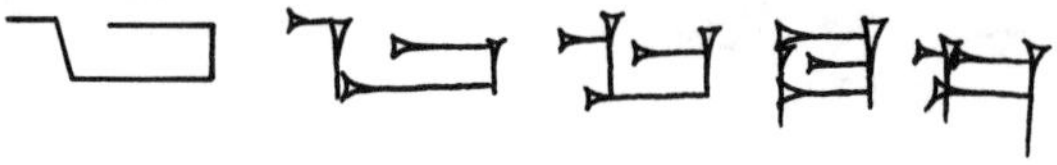	ma	 150
343		gal	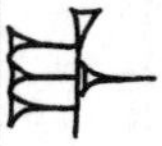 151
343		ušumgal	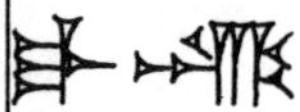 151a
344	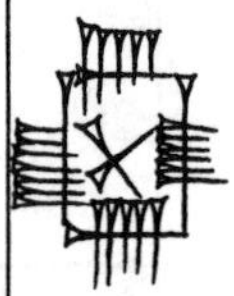	bára	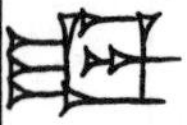 152
346		peš	 153

L				
347		niĝir	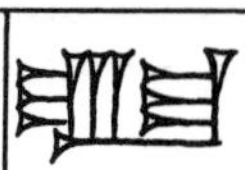	154
349		bur		155
353		ša		156
354		šu		157
354		tukumbi		157a
354b		kad_4		158
354b		kàm		158
355		ka_5 lu_5 nar		159
356	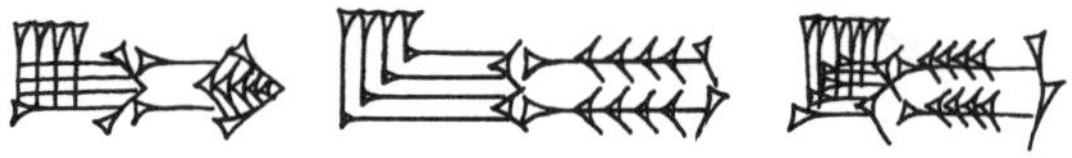	sa_6		160
358	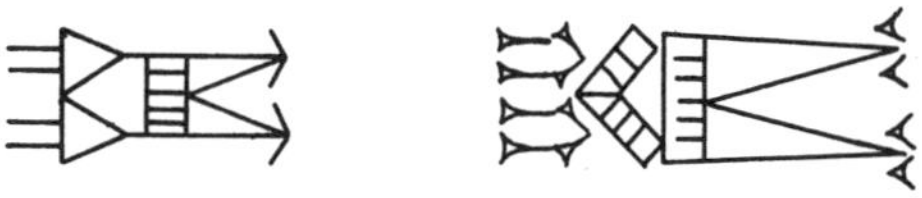	alam/n		161

L			
359		uri	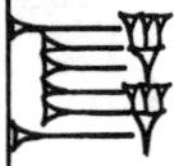 162
366		gìn kur	 163
367		še	 164
371	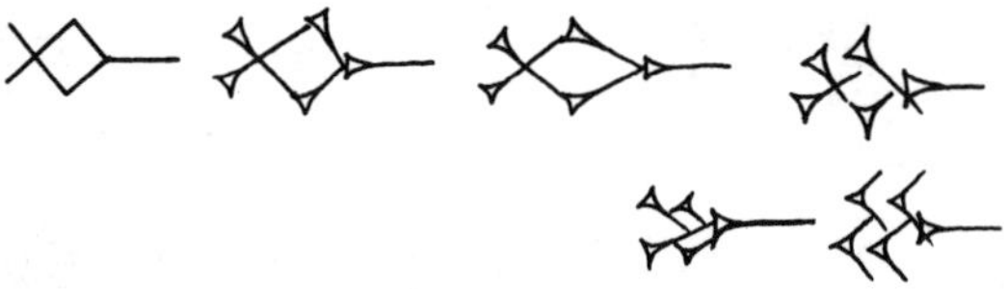	bu pu gíd sír su_{13}	 165
373		sù	 166
374		muš	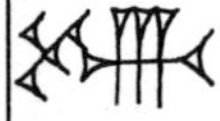 167
375	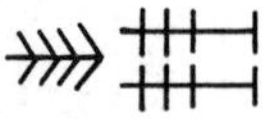	tir	 168
376		te temen	 169
376		unu_6	 169a
376*		kar	 169b

L			
381	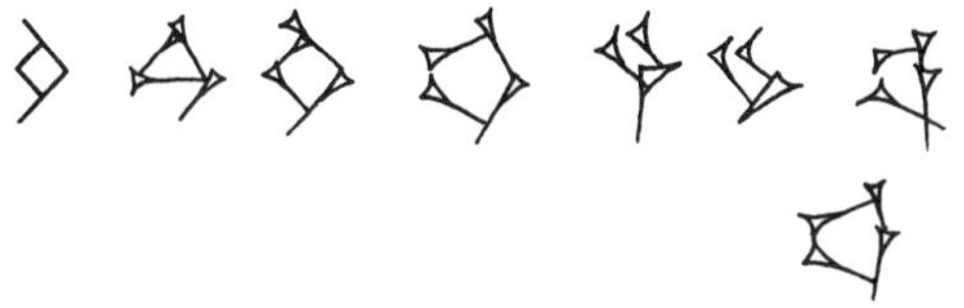	babbar bar$_6$ u$_4$ ud	 170
381		utu	 170a
381		bábbar dadag	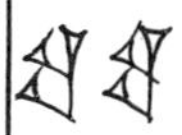 170b
381		larsa	 170c
381		è	 170d
381		zimbir	 170e
381		buranun	 170f
383		pi	 171
384		šà	 172
392		úḫ	 173
393		érin	 174
394		nunuz	 175
396		du$_{10}$ šár	 176

L			
399 399 399		im ní iškur anzu	 177  177a  177b
401		ḫur	 178
402		ḫuš	 179
406	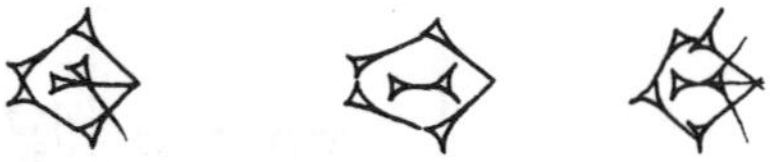	kam	 180
411	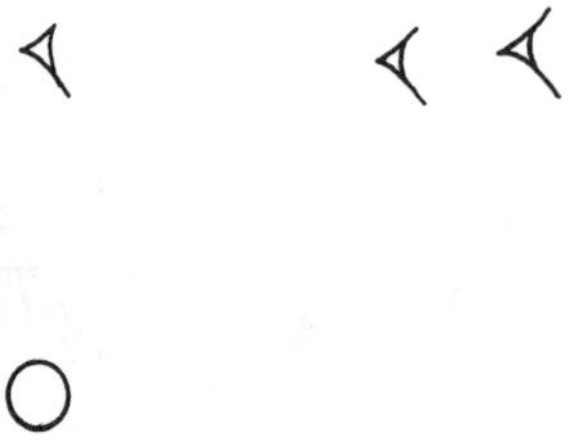	bùru u $šu_4$ šuš 10	 181
412		ugu	 182
418 418		ugun éštar	 183 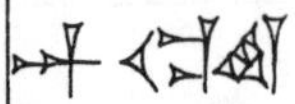 183a
420 420	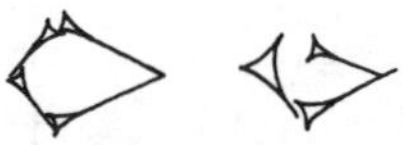	áb utul	 184  184a

L 421	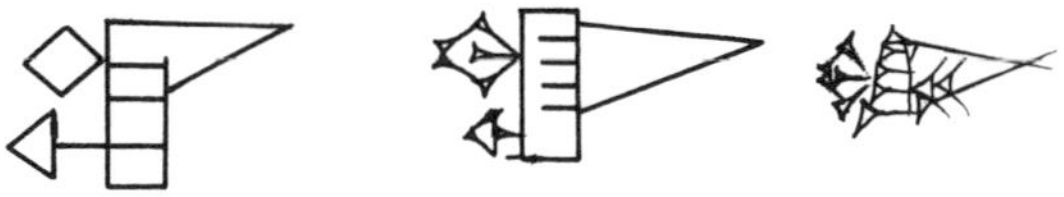	alim	 185
427	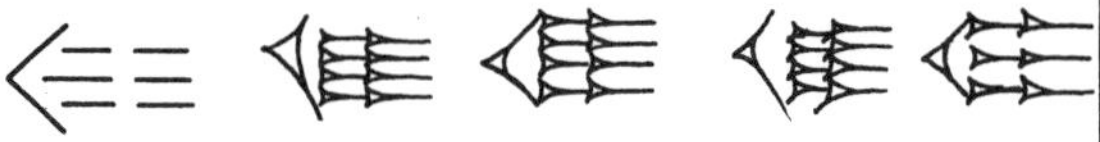	mi g̃i$_6$/gi$_6$	 186
428		šakan	 187
431	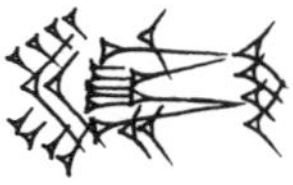	nú	 188
433		nim	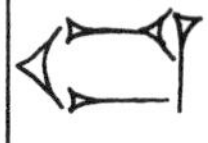 189
433		elam	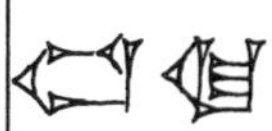 189a
434		tùm	 190
437	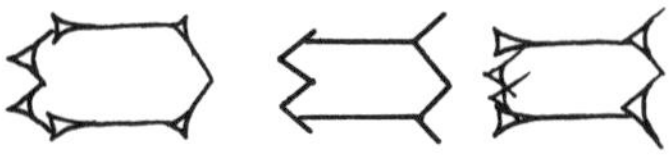	amar	 191
437		marduk	 191a
440	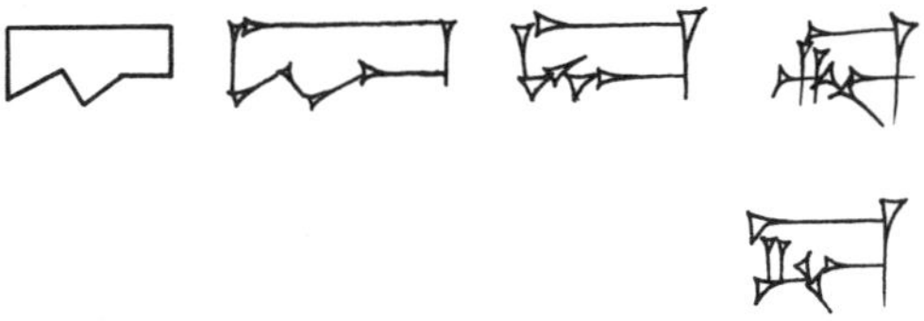	gim dím šitim	 192
441	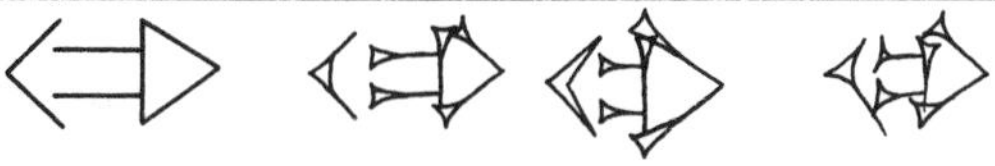	du$_7$ ul	 193

L			
445	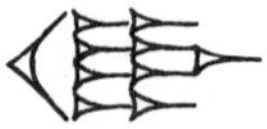	dugud	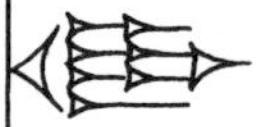 194
447a		nìgin	 195
449		gi_8 igi ši	 196
450	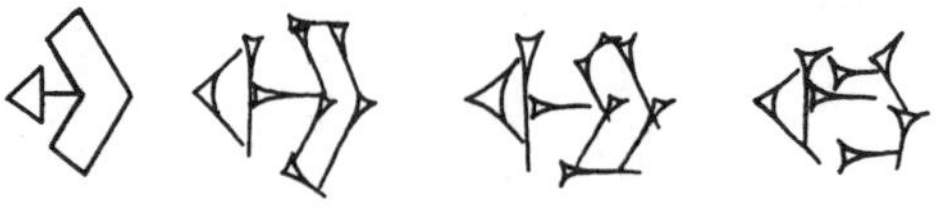	pà	 197
451		ar	 198
452	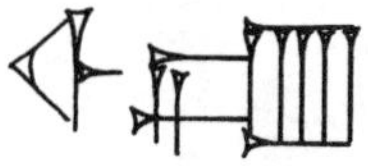	ağrig	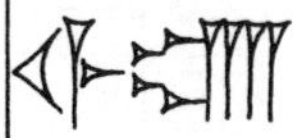 199
455	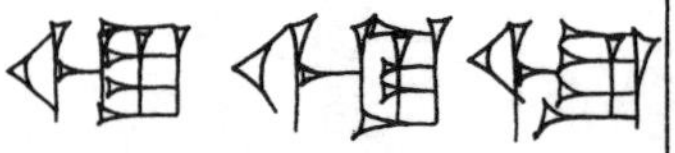	ù	 200
456		ḫul	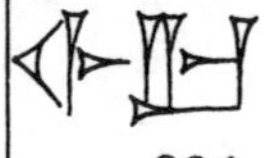 201
457	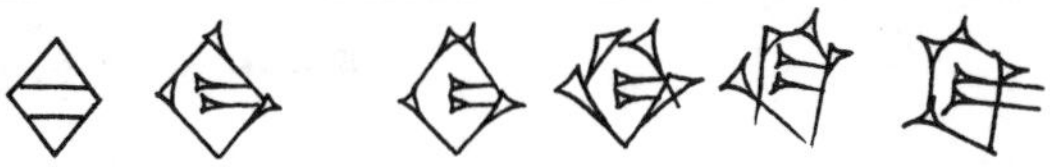	di sá silim	 202
459		dul	 203
459	 ABZ 459a	du_6	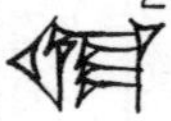 203a
459	ABZ 459a	e_{11}	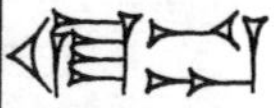 203b

L			
461	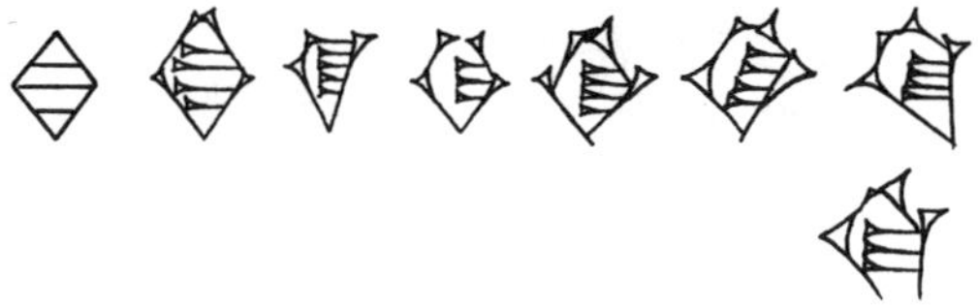	ki	 204
467	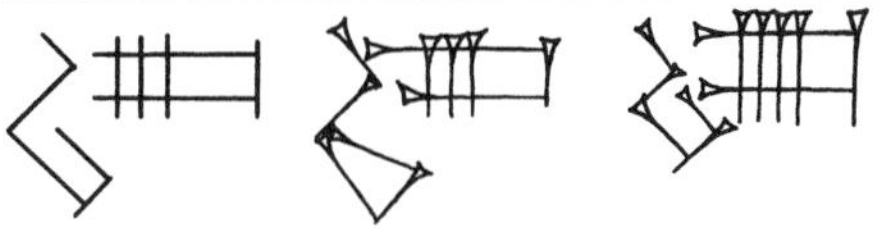	šul	 205
468		kù	 206
472		eš 30	 207
475	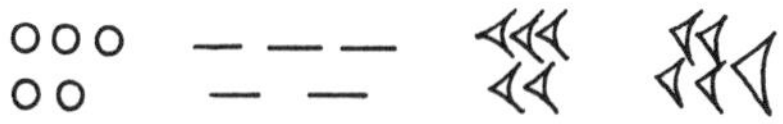	ninnu	 208
480		diš 1 ĝéš 60	 [1] 209
481		lá	 210
483		gur$_4$ niĝin ni$_{10}$	 211
484		engur nammu	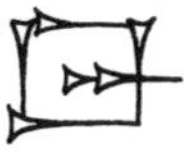 212
494		u$_8$	 213

[1] This sign is also used to indicate the name of a person.

L			
500		šára	 214
511		pú gigir	 215
522		ambar	 216
529		kìlib	 217
532		me	 218
534		g̃éš-u 600	 219
535	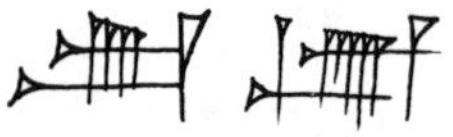	ib	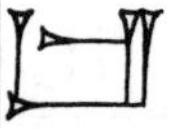 220
536	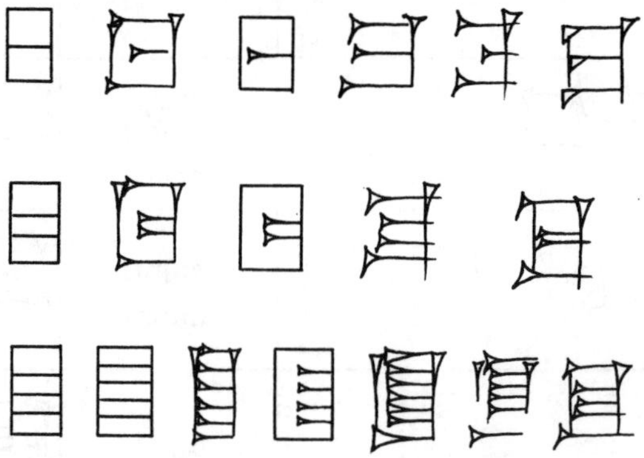	dúr dab_5 tuš[1] dul_5 éš umuš túg úb šè $durun_x$	 221  221a

[1] The readings of the signs DUR_2 / TUG_2 / $ŠE_3$ given here are those that occur in the texts in this book. For further information about how to distinguish these signs in third millennium sources see R. Biggs, JCS 20 (1966) 77, fig. 1; 77f., note 37; 87, note 101; J. Krecher, WO 18 (1987) 18f.

L			
537		udu lu	 222
538	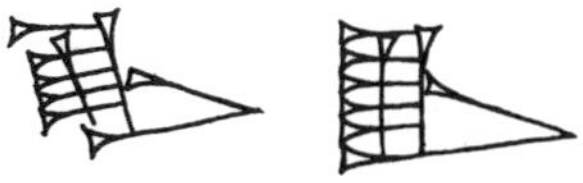	gur_{10} kí$\check{g}$	 223
539		siki	 224
541		eren	 225
545		šú	 226
546	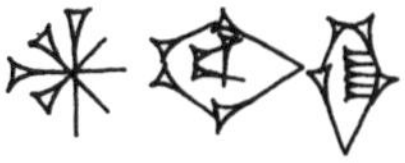	kèš	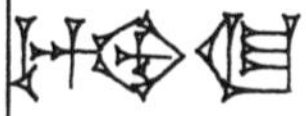 227
546		šudul	 228
554		mí gal_4 munus	 229
556		nin	 230
557		dam	 231
558		géme	 232

L 559	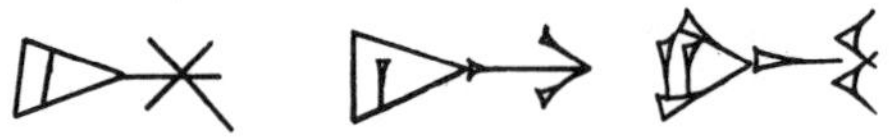	gu	 233
560		nagar	 234
562 562		kúšu umma	 235  235a
564		sikil	 236
565	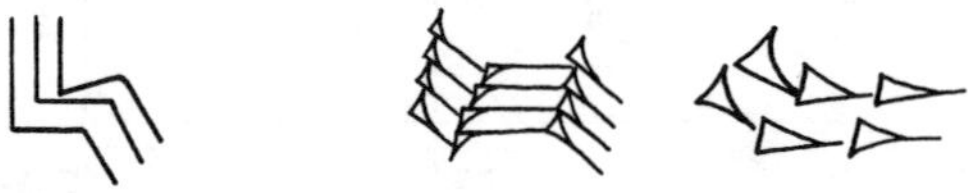	lum núm murgu	 237
567		sig_4	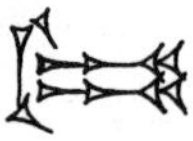 238
570		min 2	 239
571		šušana 1/3	 240
573		kingusili 5/6	 241
574		tuku	 242
575	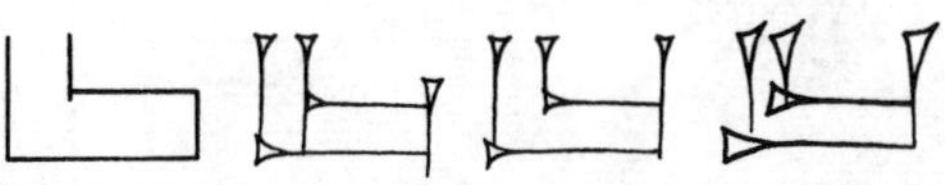	ur lik	 243

L			
579		a	 244
579		àm	 244a
579		i_7	 244b
381		buranun	 244c
586		za	 245
589		ḫa	 246
593		$eš_5$ 3	 247
595	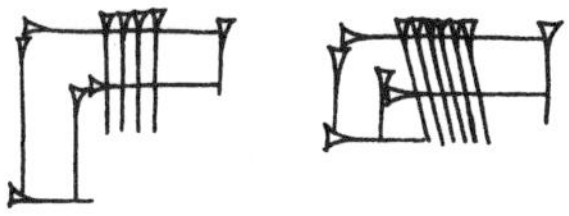	$gi\tilde{g}_4$ àga	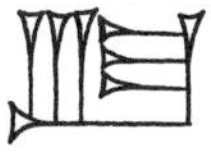 248
597		ĝar níĝ	 249
598a		ía 5	 250
598c		imin 7	 251

APPENDIX

REC SIGNS

REC 230		$utul_{12}$	252

CAPACITY MEASURES

REC 498		2 (bariga)	 253

SURFACE MEASURES

REC 509		1(bùr)	254
REC 510		10 " (=bur'u)	255
REC 511		60 "	256

PRE-SARGONIC YEAR DATES (texts 33-34 and 40-44)

	 1.(year)  2.(year) etc.	257

LIST OF PHONETIC VALUES

This List contains the phonetic values in alphabetical order. The number accompanying each phonetic value refers to the number of its sign in our sign list.

a	244
á	146
ab	70
áb	184
abzu	3a
ad	79
ág̃	94
àga	248
ag̃rig	199
ak(a)	52
akkil	49
al	125
alam/n	161
alim	185
am	91
àm	244a
am$_6$	10
ama	115
amar	191
ambar	216
an	10
anše	103
anzu	177b
ar	198
asila$_x$	83
áš	149
aša$_5$	58
ašgab	57a
ba	2
babbar	170
bábbar	170b
bàd	84
baḫar	129a
bal	6
bala	6
bànda	78
bàppir	107a
bar	37
bar$_6$	170
bára	152
bé	107
bi	107
bí	92
bu	165
bur	155
bùru	181
buranun	170f
	244c
da	147
dab$_5$	221
dadag	167b
dag	121
dag̃al	115
dam	231
dar	63
dàra	54
dé	148
dè	92
de$_6$	101
di	202
dilmun	112a
dím	192
dig̃ir	10
diri	67
diš	209
du	101
dù	111
du$_6$	203a
du$_7$	193
du$_8$	89
du$_{10}$	176
du$_{11}$	11
dub	74
dug	129
dugud	194
dul	203
dul$_5$	221
dumu	78
dur	60
dúr	221
dùr	103a
duran	60a
durun$_x$	221a
e	128
é	138
è	170d
e$_{11}$	203b
eden	90
elam	189a
en	53
èn	25
engar	22
engur	212
énsi	122d
èr	17
eren	225
eridu	47a
érim	92a
érin	174
esag̃$_x$	138a
esi	137a
eš	207
éš	221
èš	70
eš$_5$	247
éštar	183a
ezem/n	82
ga	134
g̃á	114
gada	48
gag	111
gal	151
g̃ál	42
gal$_4$	229
gala	105a
g̃alga	120
gan	77
gána	58
g̃anun	116
g̃ar	249
gára	134a
gàr	145
ge	45
ge$_4$	140
g̃e$_{26}$	114
géme	232
g̃en	101
g̃éš	209
g̃éš-u	219
g̃eštin	104
g̃éštu	123b
g̃èštu	123c

gi	45
gi$_{4}$	140
gi$_{6}$	186
g̃i$_{6}$	186
gi$_{8}$	196
gi$_{16}$	30
gibil	93
gíd	165
g̃idru	122
gig̃$_{4}$	248
gígir	215
gim	192
gìn	163
g̃ír	7
giri$_{17}$	11
g̃iš	123
gišgal	16b
gu	233
gú	59
gù	11
gu$_{4}$	124
gu$_{7}$	12
g̃u$_{10}$	27
gub	101
gum	96
gunu$_{4}$	97
gur	61
gùr	135
gur$_{4}$	211
gur$_{8}$	24
gur$_{10}$	223
gur$_{11}$	134
g̃uruš	137

ḫa	246
ḫé	77
ḫu	40
ḫul	201
ḫur	178
ḫuš	179

i	76
ì	112
i$_{7}$	244b
ía	250
ib	220
íb	102
íbila	78a
ig	42
igi	196
íl	135
im	177
imin	251
in	80
inanna	56a
inim	11
ir	113
iri	13
iš	106
iškur	177a
ištaran	11a
iti	19
izi	92

ka	11
ká	72
ka$_{5}$	159
kad$_{4}$	158
kala	137
kalam	130
kam	180
kàm	158
kar	169b
kár	58
kas	88
kas$_{4}$	100
ke$_{4}$	131
kéš	85
kèš	227
ki	204
kib	109
kíg̃	223
kìlib	217
kingusili	241
kiri$_{6}$	123a
kisal	117
kù	206
ku$_{4}$	24
ku$_{5}$	9
kur	163
kúr	26
kuš	4
kuš$_{7}$	106
kúšu	235

la	21
lá	210
lagaš/s	34a
laḫ$_{5}$	101a
larsa	170c
le	25
li	25
lí	112
li$_{9}$	92
lik	243
líl	131
límmu	68
lu	222
lú	142
lu$_{5}$	159
lugal	81
luḫ	136
lum	237

ma	150
má	65
maḫ	23
mar	127
marduk	191a
maš	37
máš	39
maškim	122b
me	218
mi	186
mí	229
min	239
mu	27
mú	86
mul	71
mun	51
munus	229
murgu	237
muš	167
mùš	56
mušen	40

na	33
na$_{4}$	110
nagar	234
nam	41
nammu	212
nanna	143c
nanše	98
nar	159
ne	92
né	112
ni	112
ní	177
ni$_{10}$	211
níg̃	249
níg̃in	211
nìgin	195
nig̃ir	154
nim	189
nin	230
nina	98a
ninnu	208
nir	139
nita	105
nu	38
nú	188
núm	237
numun	35
nun	47
nunuz	175

pa	122
pà	197
pa$_5$	26a
par$_4$	117
peš	153
pi	171
pu	165
pú	215
ra	141
rá	101
re	46
re$_6$	101
ri	46
rí	13
rig$_7$	122a
ru	31
rú	111
rum	1
sa	57
sá	202
sa$_4$	43
sa$_6$	160
sa$_{10}$	95
sağ	64
sagi	28a
saḫar	106
sağğa	132
sám	95
sar	86
sè	87
si	62
sig$_4$	238
sig$_{15}$	137
sig$_{17}$	45
siki	224
sikil	236
sila	9
sìla	28
sila$_4$	118
silim	202
sîn	53a
sipa	122e
sír	165
su	4
sú	3
sù	166
su$_{13}$	165
su'en	53a
suḫuš	99
sukkal	136
sur	55
ša	156
šà	172
šab	122c
šakan	187
šár	176
šára	214
še	164
šè	221
šen	5
šeš	143
ši	196
šim	108
šir	34
šita	114a
šitim	192
šu	157
šú	226
šu$_4$	181
šub	31
šub$_5$	44a
šùba	56b
šubur	20
šudul	228
šul	205
šúm	87
šur	55
šuš	181
šušana	240
ta	75
tag	69
taka$_4$	29
tar	9
te	169
temen	169
ti	36
til	32
tir	168
tu	24
túg	221
tuku	242
tukumbi	157a
túm	101
tùm	190
tuš	221
u	181
ú	133
ù	200
u$_4$	170
u$_8$	213
u$_{18}$	16b
ub	126
úb	221
ud	170
ud$_5$	66
udu	222
ùğ	130
uğ$_5$	84
ugu	182
ugula	122
ugun	183
úḫ	173
ul	193
um	73
umbin	50
umma	235a
umuš	221
un	130
unken	14
unu$_6$	169a
unug	97a
ur	243
ùr	119
úrdu	18
uri	162
úri	143a
uri$_5$	143b
urin	143
uru	13
uru$_{12}$	119
uru$_{16}$	53
URUxA	16a
uru$_x$	15
ús	105
uš	105
ušum	8
ušumgal	151a
utu	170a
utul	184a
utul$_{12}$	252
za	245
zà	144
zal	112
zi	44
zimbir	170e
zu	3
zú	11

GLOSSARY

This glossary is divided into the following parts:

General Vocabulary
Divine Names
Personal Names
Place Names
Sacred Buildings
Year Dates
Year Names
Festivals

The *General Vocabulary* contains the words that appear in the texts contained in this book. It does not claim to.give a detailed definition of each word, but rather the general sense. Particular meanings are given only when they are necessary to understand a particular passage; in such a case the passage in question is indicated. Grammatical elements are not included among the words that are defined.

The Akkadian equivalents, when known, are placed next to each Sumerian word: naturally, the Akkadian words themselves do not appear in the Sumerian texts. On the other hand, Sumerian equivalents are placed next to each Akkadian word in the Akkadian glossary.

Within the General Vocabulary the following grammatical terms and abbreviations are used:

ḫamṭu / marû: for a discussion of these Akkadian grammatical terms that are used to describe aspects of the Sumerian verb, see P. Attinger, Éléments de linguistique sumérienne. La construction de du$_{11}$/e/di «dire» (Orbis Biblicus et Orientalis, Sonderband; Fribourg/Göttingen 1993), § 119 and § 120.

R = word root

cf. (confer) is a way of indicating that the Akkadian represents an equivalent, although such an equation does not explicitly appear in the ancient texts. It also indicates a semantic relationship rather than a translation.

GENERAL VOCABULARY

SUMERIAN

a (*mû*)	water
(amar-)a-a-si-ge$_4$-da	see amar-R-R-si-ge$_4$-da
a-ga (cf. *warkatum*)	back room
a-ra-zu (*teslītum*)	prayer
a-rá (*adi / -ī-šu*)	x times
a--ru (*šarākum*)	to dedicate
á (*idum*)	arm; strength; power; rent (31:2)
á--ág̃ (*wârum* D)	to give a command or an instruction

á-...-ta	at the prompting of; by means of the strength of
áb (*littum*)	cow
abzu (*apsûm*)	see *Sacred Buildings*
ad-da (*abum*)	father
á$\tilde{g}$ (*madādum*)	to measure (by means of a measure of capacity)
(á--)á$\tilde{g}$	see á--R
(ki(-g)--)á$\tilde{g}$	see ki--R
àga-kár--sè(-g)	to strike with a weapon; to conquer (see J. Klein, Studies Tadmor, 310f.)
àga-ús (*rēdûm*)	policeman
a$\tilde{g}$rig (*abarakkum*)	steward; an important temple administrator
AK (*epēšum*)	to do; for the different readings of AK see A. Cavigneaux, SAZ, 45-47; M. Powell, Studies Diakonoff, 314-319
(ní$\tilde{g}$--)ak-(ak)	see ní$\tilde{g}$--R-(R)
(šu-gibil--)ak	see šu-gibil--R
akkil (*ikkillum*)	lamentation
al (*allum*)	hoe; see note to zú
alam/n (*ṣalmum*)	statue
alim (*ditānum, kusarikkum*)	bison
ama (*ummum*)	mother
ama-ar-gi$_8$ (*andurārum*)	freedom$^?$ (gi$_8$ is a graphic variant of gi$_4$); lit.: to return to mother, cf. G. Farber, AulOr 9 (1991) 87
amar (*būrum*)	calf; a young animal
amar-a-a-si-ge$_4$-da	see *Festivals*
ambar (*appārum*)	swamp; canebrake. The reading /ambar/ is conventional; according to PEa 42 (and other sources) it should rather be /abbar/; see J. Krecher, AOAT 1 (1969) 171, note 20
an (*šamû*)	heaven; sky
an-ub-da (*kibrātum*)	regions; "quarter"
anše (*imērum*)	donkey
asila$_x$ [EZENxSILA$_{11}$] (*rīštum*)	joy
aša$_5$(-g) (*eqlum*)	a plot of land; see GANA$_2$
ašgab (*aškāpum*)	leatherworker

ba (*qiāšum*)	to donate
(šu--)ba	see šu--R
ba-al (*ḫerûm*)	to dig a canal; to channel
babbar / bábbar (*namrum; peṣûm*)	shining; white
(kù-)bábbar	see kù-R
bàd (*dūrum*)	wall

(sig$_4$-)báḫar	see sig$_4$-R
bala (*palûm*)	term of office; reign; dynasty
(nu-)bànda	see nu-R
(é-)bàppir	see *Sacred Buildings*
(lú-)bàppir	see lú-R
bar (igi-g̃ál-ni)	see note to igi-g̃ál
(igi--)bar	see igi--R
(igi-zi--)bar	see igi-zi--R
bariga ('UL'; *pars/šiktum*)	a measure of capacity (ca. 60 l.; cf. RlA 7, 492ff.; 497 § IV.5)
-bi-da(-ke$_4$) (*u*)	and
bùr (*būrum*)	a surface measure (loan from the Akkadian): 1 bùr = 3 eše = 18 iku = 1800 s/šar (see RlA 7, 480f. § II.11)
bùru(-d) (*palāšum*)	to pierce
da(-g)	nearness (to someone; see J. Krecher, ASJ 9 [1987] 88, note 39)
dab$_5$ (*ṣabātum*)	to seize; to take; to take away
(di--)dab$_5$	see di--R
dadag (*namrum*)	pure; shining; bright
(g̃á-la--)dag	see g̃á-la--R
dag̃al 1. (*rapšum*)	wide
2. (*rapāšum* D)	to broaden
(šu-)dag̃al--(du$_{11}$)	see šu-R--du$_{11}$
dam (*aššatum*)	wife
(kù-)dam-(tak$_4$)	see kù-R-tak$_4$
dam-gàr (*tamkārum*)	merchant (loan from the Akkadian); for the reading dam-gàra instead of dam-gàr, see J. Bauer, ZA 61 (1971) 317ff.
(^{d}nin-)dar	see *Divine Names*
dàra (*turāḫum*)	mountain goat; the reading dàra is conventional, see P. Steinkeller, SEL 6 (1989) 3-7
(má-)dàra-(abzu)	see má-R-abzu
(gù--)dé	see gù--R
de$_6$	see DU
di (*qabûm*) [*marû* participle of du$_{11}$(-g)]	to say; to speak
di--dab$_5$ (*dīnam šūḫuzum*)	to take up a lawsuit; for a discussion of this term see E. Dombradi, FAOS 20/1, § 224 and § 421-423
di-ku$_5$ 1. (*dajjānum*)	judge

2. (*dīnum*)	judgment
di--ku$_5$(-d^r) (*dīnam diānum*)	to pass judgment
di-til-la (*dīnum gamrum*)	law case for which a final decision has been given
diĝir 1. (*ilum*)	god; divinity
2.	determinative for divine beings
dím (*epēšum*)	to build; to make
(kù-)dím	see kù-R
diri-...-šè	beyond
diš (*ištēn*)	one
du (*alākum* [*marû*])	to go
DU [*ḫamṭu*: de$_6$; *marû*: túm]	
1. (*wabālum*)	to bring; to deliver
2. (*tabālum*)	to carry off; to take along
(šu-du$_8$-a--)DU	see šu-du$_8$-a--R
DU.DU	see laḫ$_5$
du-rí (*dārûm*)	everlasting; enduring
(mun-)du	see mun-R
dù [*d^{r}u] (*banûm; epēšum*)	to build; to construct; to erect (for dù/rú = d^{r}u see P. Steinkeller, JCS 35 [1983] 249f.)
(ĝír--)dù	see ĝír--R
(ĝiš--)dù	see ĝiš--R
du$_7$ (*wasmum*)	fitting; suitable; necessary
(ḫé-)du$_7$	see ḫé-R
(šu--)du$_7$	see šu--du$_7$
du$_8$ 1. (*labānum*)	to spread; to mould bricks ; öffnen (z.B. Augen)
2. (*peḫûm*)	to coat with pitch; to caulk
(šu-)du$_8$-(a--DU)	see šu-R-a--DU
(igi-nu-)du$_8$	see igi-nu-R
du$_{10}$(-g) (*ṭābum*)	good; favorable; pleasing
du$_{11}$(-g) (*qabûm; dabābum* [*ḫamṭu*])	to say; to declare
(sá--)du$_{11}$-du$_{11}$	see sá--R-R
(šu-daĝal--)du$_{11}$	see šu-daĝal--R
(šu-tag--)du$_{11}$	see šu-tag--R
du$_{11}$-ga (*qibītum*)	utterance; speech (29:7)
dub (*ṭ/tuppum*)	tablet; document
(saĝ-)dub	see note to saĝ-R
DUB.ŠEN	a type of chest that serves as a treasure-box (see J. Bauer, AoN 1985, 20ff., n. 29)
dug (*karpatum*)	jug; vessel
(èš-)DUG.(RU)	see *Sacred Buildings*
dugud (*kabtum*)	heavy; important
dul (*katāmum*)	to cover

dul$_5$ (*katāmum*)	to cover (dul$_5$ is the graph used in Pre-Sargonic texts such as in 18 ii 4. It is later replaced by dul)
dumu 1. (*mārum*)	child; son
2. (*mārtum*)	daughter
dumu-KA	grandson (see Å. Sjöberg, HSAO, 209f.)
dumu-mí (*mārtum*)	daughter
dumu-tu-da	son of (lit.: son born (of)); see note to tu(-d)
^{ĝiš}dúr-ĝar (*kussûm; durga(r)rû*)	chair; throne (see H. Waetzoldt, RlA 8, 327f., § 5.2)
dùr (*mūrum*)	foal
dùr-KAS$_4$ (*šānûm*)	donkey foal (the reading of KAS$_4$ is uncertain, cf. MSL VIII/1, 52: 380-381)
durun$_x$(DUR$_2$.DUR$_2$)	to place (objects [15 iii 3]); for DUR$_2$.DUR$_2$ = durun$_x$ (plural form of the verb tuš) see P. Steinkeller, OrNS 48 (1979) 55f., note 6
(ú-)durun$_x$(DUR$_2$.DUR$_2$)	see ú-R
e (*qabûm* [*marû*])	to say; see du$_{11}$(-g)
é (*bītum*)	house; temple (see the names in *Sacred Buildings*); plot of land
é-gal (*ekallum*)	palace
é-mí	women's residence (see K. Maekawa, Mesopotamia 8/9 [1973-1974] 77ff.)
è [*ḫamṭu*; *marû*: è(-d)] (*waṣûm* G, Š)	to (let) go out; to come out; to lead out; to bring out; to appear (as a witness)
(pa--)è	see pa--R
e$_{11}$(-d) (*warādum* Š)	to bring down; to fetch
eden (*edinu; ṣērum*)	steppe; plain
(gú-)eden-(na)	see gú-R-na
en 1. (*enum*)	a kind of priest; a partner in the sacred marriage
2. (*bēlum*)	lord
(ki-)en-(gi(-r))	see ki-R-gi(-r)
en-nu-uĝ$_5$ (*maṣṣartum*)	guard; watchpost (the reading en-nu-uĝ$_5$ (not /-ug$_5$/) is confirmed by MSL XII, 101:167; 116:14 contrary to J. Krecher, Studies Matouš II, 37)
(saĝ-)èn-(tar)	see saĝ-R-tar
engar (*ikkarum*)	farmer
engar-gu$_4$-ra	farmer (and) oxherd (see H. Steible, FAOS 9/2, 54f.)
énsi (*iššiakkum*)	city ruler
énsi-gal	a kind of priest(?)
$^{\text{(ĝiš)}}$eren (*erēnum*)	cedar(wood)

eren-bábbar (*ti(')āl/rum*)	white cedar(wood)
(nam-)érim	see nam-R
(nam-)érim--(ku$_5$(-d^r))	see nam-R--ku$_5$(-d^r)
(nam-)érin	see nam-R
esaĝ$_x$ (E$_2$.ŠE) (*qarītum*)	storeroom; for E$_2$.ŠE = a/esaĝ$_x$ see J. Krecher, Studies Matouš II, 36; Å. Sjöberg, ZA 83 (1993) 15f.
^{na4}esi (*ušûm*)	diorite (as in (all?) of Gudea's statues); olivine-gabbro (see W. Heimpel, RA 76 [1982] 65ff; ZA 77 [1987] 48f.)
eš (= eš$_5$; *šalāš*)	three (36:4)
èš (*bītum*)	sanctuary (see CAD B, 282, lexical section)
eš$_5$ (*šalāš*)	three
ezem/n (*isinnum*)	festival; feast. The reading ezem/n is conventional; for /izim/ or /izin/ in OB and pre-OB sources, see Å. Sjöberg, ZA 83 (1993) 15; P. Steinkeller, Studies Hallo, 245. For particulars about the festivals that appear in texts 41-44, see the information in *Festivals*
ga (*šizbum*)	milk (see M. Stol, RlA 8, 189ff.)
ĝá-la--dag (*naparkûm*)	to stop working
^{d}ĝá-tùm-du$_{10}$(-g)	see *Divine Names*
ĝá-^{ĝiš}ù-šub-ba (*nalbanum*)	brick making shed (see D.A. Foxvog, N.A.B.U. 1998/7)
(na-)gada	see na-R
^{ĝiš}gag-si-sá (*šiltāḫum*)	arrow
gal 1. (*rabûm*)	big; mighty; great
2.	chief (34 vi 4)
gal-zu (*mūdûm*)	wise; intelligent
(é-)gal	see é-R
(énsi-)gal	see énsi-R
ĝál--taka$_4$ (*petûm*)	to open
(igi-(x-))ĝál	see igi-(x-)R
(nir-)ĝál	see nir-R
(zi-)ĝál-(la)	see zi-R-la
(giri$_{17}$-šu--)ĝál	see giri$_{17}$-šu--R
(gú-ĝiš--)ĝál	see gú-ĝiš--R
(zi-šà-)ĝál	see zi-šà-R
gal$_4$(-la) (*ūrum*)	female sexual organs; vulva (/-la/ in gal$_4$-la /*galla/ is a phonetic complement)

gala (*kalûm*)	liturgical singer (see J. Krecher, SKLy, 27f., 35f.); the archaic spelling of gala was ĜIŠ$_3$.DUR$_2$ 'penis + anus' (see P. Steinkeller / J.N. Postgate, MC 4, 37)
ĝalga (*milkum*)	advice
gan (*wālittum*)	said about females: "which bore or can bear"
(má-)gan	see má-R^{ki}
GANA$_2$ (*eqlum*)	a plot of land; for GANA$_2$(-g) = aša$_5$(-g) see M. Civil, JCS 25 (1973) 171ff. and M. Powell, ibid., 178ff.
ĝanun (*ganūnum*)	storehouse; granary
ĝar (*šakānum*)	to set; to put
(^{ĝiš}dúr-)ĝar	see ^{ĝiš}dúr-R
(igi--)ĝar	see igi--R
(NE.NE-)ĝar	see NE.NE-R
(sá-)ĝar	see sá-R
(dam-)gàr	see dam-R
ĝen (*alākum* [*ḫamṭu*, singular])	to go
ĝéš (*šūši*)	sixty
ĝéš-u (*nēru*)	six hundred
ĝeštin (*karānum*)	grape juice; bunch of grapes
ĝéštu(-g) / ĝèštu(-g) 1. (*uznum*)	ear
2. (*ḫasīsum*)	understanding; wisdom
gi (*apum; qanûm*)	reed
gi-gù-na (*gigunûm*)	a sacred building ('reed chamber'; see *Sacred Buildings*)
gi-gunu$_4$	a sacred building ('reed chamber'), see gi-gù-na
gi (-n // gi-in) (*kânum* G, D)	to be firm; to make firm; to be steadfast; to be stable; to fix; to award; with ka-g.a: to agree with a statement
(ki-en-)gi(-r)	see ki-en-R
gi$_4$ (*târum* G, D)	to return; to bring back; to take a case up again
(ki-bi--)gi$_4$-(gi$_4$)	see ki-bi--R-R
(šu--)gi$_4$	see šu--R
gi$_6$(-g) (*ṣalmum*)	dark
(kas-)gi$_6$	see kas-R
ĝi$_6$-par$_4$ (*gipa(r)ru*)	dwelling of the en-priest or en-priestess
(ama-ar-)gi$_8$	see ama-ar-R
gi$_{16}$-sa (*dārûm, dārītum*)	lasting; of lasting value
(šu-)gibil--(AK)	see šu-R--AK
gíd (*šadādum*)	to drag; to tow; to measure; to manage (38:7)
(má-)gíd	see má-R
ĝidru (*ḫaṭṭum*)	scepter

gíĝ$_4$ (*šiqlum*)	shekel (a unit of weight, ca. 8, 333 gr.; see M. Powell, RlA 7, 510 § V.4)
^{giš}gígir (*narkabtum*)	wagon; chariot
-gim (*kīma*)	like
ĝír--DU$_3$	to cut off(?)
(^{d}nin-)ĝír-(su$_{1/2}$)	see *Divine Names*
giri$_{17}$ (*appum*)	nose; the conventional reading /kìri/ is most likely appropriate only for texts from northern Babylonia (Kiš, Sippar(?), cf. MSL XIV, 110, 1.1 i' 4'; VS 10 101 rev. 1), whereas PEa Nippur indicates a reading /giri/ (= giri$_{17}$), cf. PEa 305; 418
giri$_{17}$-šu--ĝál (*appam labānum*)	to greet and entreat (lit.: to let the hand be at the nose; see U. Magen, BaF 9 (1986) 60-61; 104-108)
ĝiš 1. (*iṣum*)	tree; wood
2.	determinative for wooden objects; the reading ĝiš is conventional; lexical (PEa 641) and other sources indicate a reading ĝeš
ĝiš-dù-a	timber (see H. Steible, FAOS 9/2, 43f.)
ĝiš--ḫur (*eṣērum*)	to make a drawing; to design
ĝiš-ḫur (*uṣurtum; gišḫu(r)ru*)	cultic rule or ordinance (cf. G. Farber-Flügge, St. Pohl 10, 181f.; AulOr 9 [1991] 85f.)
ĝiš-kíĝ-ti (*kiška/ittû*)	craftsman
ĝiš-nú (*eršum*)	bed; see H. Waetzoldt, RlA 8, 326f.; for ĜIŠ.NU$_2$ = ĝi/ešna/u$_x$ see J. Krecher, Studies Matous II, 48
ĝiš--tag (cf. *gištaggû*)	to offer
(gú-)ĝiš--(ĝál)	see gú-R--ĝál
(ì-)ĝiš	see ì-R
^{giš}gu-za (*kussûm*)	throne; chair (see H. Waetzoldt, RlA 8, 327f.)
gu-za-lá (*guzalûm*)	chair-bearer; throne-bearer
gú-ĝiš--ĝál	to provide a delivery of wood
gù--dé (*nabûm*)	to call; to name
gu$_4$ (-d^r) (*alpum*)	steer; ox
(engar)-gu$_4$-(ra)	see engar-R-ra
gu$_7$ (*akālum*)	to eat; to suck (milk); to enjoy the usufruct of something
(níĝ-)gu$_7$-(a)	see níĝ-R-a
-ĝu$_{10}$ (*-ī/-ja*)	my
gub (*izuzzum* G, Š)	to stand; to set up
(gi-)gù-n(a)	see gi-R
(gi-)gunu$_4$	see gi-R
gur (*târum* G, D)	to return; to give back
(má-)gur$_8$	see má-R

(še-)gur$_{10}$--(ku$_{5}$)	see še-R--ku$_{5}$
(níĝ-)gur$_{11}$	see níĝ-R
ĝuruš (*eṭlum*)	an adult; young man; recruit; worker

(ne-)ḫa	see ne-R
ḫa-la (*zittum*)	lot; assigned portion
ḫa-lu-úb (*ḫa/uluppum*)	oak(?) (see BSA 3, 135; 146; BSA 6, 159; 182)
ḫé-du$_{7}$ (*wusmum*)	decoration
ḫé-ĝál (*ḫe(n)gallum; ṭuḫdum*)	overflow; abundance
ḫul (*šulputum*)	to destroy; to ruin; for a discussion of the verb /ḫul/<->/ḫulu/ see J. Krecher, AOAT 240, 192f., with note 103
(ĝiš-)ḫur	see ĝiš-R
(ĝiš--)ḫur	see ĝiš--R
ḫur-saĝ (*ḫuršānum*)	hill country; mountainous region
ḫuš (*ḫuššûm; ruššûm*)	red; terrifying

i (= è)	to come out; to appear (in the phrase u$_{4}$-ul-lí-a-ta); there seems to be a semantic relation between /i/ and /è/, but it is uncertain whether /i/ and /è/ can be considered as identical verbs
ì (*šamnum*)	vegetable oil; animal fat
ì-bí-la (*aplum*)	heir (syllabic writing of ibila)
ì-du$_{8}$ (*atûm*)	porter; door keeper
ì-ĝiš (*ellum; šamnum*)	sesame oil
i$_{7}$(-d) 1. (*nārum*)	river; canal
2.	determinative for rivers and canals
ía (*ḫamiš*)	five
íbila (*aplum*)	heir (loan from the Akkadian?)
ig (*daltum*)	(panel of a) door
igi (*īnum*)	eye; glance
igi-...-šè (*maḫar*)	in the presence of (said about witnesses at a trial)
igi--bar (*amārum; naplusum*)	to look at (see J. Krecher, Kutscher Memorial Vol., 108ff.)
igi-(x-)ĝál	a phrase used to express fractions (see J. Friberg, RlA 7, 535f. § 3.1); the phrase bar igi-ĝál-ni (38:5) is difficult to define
igi--ĝar	to appear before someone (37:3); for this use of igi--ĝar, corresponding to the Akkadian *pānī šakānum*, see E. Dombradi, FAOS 20/1, § 402

igi-nu-du$_8$(-a)	helper; unskilled worker (see G.J. Selz, FAOS 15/1, 72 1:1)
igi-zi--bar (*kīniš naplusum*)	to choose; to legitimate (lit.: to look on favorably)
íl (*našûm*)	to lift; to bring, to convey; to endure
(sag̃--)íl	see sag̃--R
im (*ṭīdum*)	clay; loam
imin (*sebe*)	seven (<*ía-min, 5+2)
inim (*awātum*)	word; statement; decree
inim-ma--sè(-g)	to imagine (lit.: to place in a word; see M. Civil, Studies Birot, 75)
(lú-)inim-(ma)	see lú-R-ma
(lú-ki-)inim-(ma)	see lú-ki-R-ma
ir (*erī/ēšum*)	fragrance; perfume; fragrant
iri 1. (*ālum*)	city; district
2.	determinative for cities
iti (*warḫum*)	month (for the individual month names see the index in M.E. Cohen, Cultic Calendars, 483ff.)
izi (*išātum*)	fire
izi--lá	to purify with fire (see J. Bauer, AfO 40/41 [1993/94] 95; for a reading bí--lá, to spread smoke, see J. Krecher, OrNS 54 [1985] 147, note 31)
ka-al(-ak) (cf. *kalakkum*)	loam pit (23 ii 22; 25 ii 14; see D.A. Foxvog, N.A.B.U. 1998/7)
ka(-g) (*pûm*)	statement (in the expression ka.g- ... -a--gi(-n) [37:11; 38:29]; see J. Krecher, ZA 69 [1979] 1-3)
ka-šakan	chief oil-maker (see P. Steinkeller, FAOS 17, 200, and (ka-)šakan below)
(dumu-)KA	see dumu-R
ká (*bābum*)	gate
kala(-g) (*dannum*)	strong; mighty
kalam (*mātum*)	land (specifically, Sumer)
kàm (*nakārum* D)	to overturn; to change (29:7)
kar (*kārum*)	quay
(àga-)kár--(sè(-g))	see àga-R--sè(-g)
kas (*šika/ārum*)	beer (fermented barley); alcoholic beverage (see CAD Š/II, 428, discussion section)
kas-gi$_6$(-g)	dark beer
kas-sig$_{15}$	light beer (see M. Powell, HANE/S 6, 104ff.)
(dùr-)KAS$_4$	see dùr-R
kéš(-d^r) (*keš(e)d^r/*kšed^r) (*rakāsum*)	to bind (see A. Cavigneaux/F. Al-Rawi, ZA 85 [1995] 36, note 8)

(zú--)kéš(-d^{r})	see zú--R
ki 1. (*ašrum*)	place; location; area; world
2.	determinative for place names
ki-...-ta	disbursed by (lit.: from the place of)
ki-bi--gi$_{4}$-(gi$_{4}$) (*ana ašrīšu turrum*)	to restore (lit.: to return to its place)
ki-en-gi(-r; *kenĝir)	the land of Sumer (what the Sumerians called their land); see *Place Names*
(lú-)ki-(inim-ma)	see lú-R-inim-ma
ki-tuš (*šubtum*)	dwelling
ki-uri	the land of Akkade (uri <**war*(*i*); what the Sumerians called Akkade); see *Place Names*
ki(-g)--áĝ 1. (*râmum*)	to love; to show affection
2. (*narāmum*)	beloved
(ĝiš-)kíĝ-(ti)	see ĝiš-R-ti
kìlib (*napḫarum*)	totality
kingusili (*parasrab*)	five-sixths
(nu-)kiri$_{6}$(-k)	see nu-R
kisal (*kisallum*)	courtyard
kiši$_{4}$ (*muttatum*)	half (in 39:21 it refers to the hair of the head)
kù(-g) 1. (*elēlum* D)	to purify; to make culticly pure
2. (*ellum*)	pure; holy
3. (*kaspum*)	silver
kù-bábbar (*kaspum*)	silver
kù-dam-taka$_{4}$ (*uzubbûm*)	divorce-settlement
kù-dím (*kuttimmum*)	silversmith
kù-luḫ (*kaspum mesûm*)	refined silver
kù-sig$_{17}$ (*ḫurāṣum*)	gold (see Å. Sjöberg, JCS 40 [1988] 174)
(ù--)ku$_{4}$	see ù--R (this verbal root must be distinguished from ku$_{4}$(-r) because it can appear as ù--ku)
ku$_{4}$(-r <d^{r}) (*erēbum* G, Š)	to (let) enter; to bring in (see J. Krecher, ZA 77 [1987] 7ff.)
ku$_{5}$(-d^{r}) (*nakāsum*)	to cut
(di-)ku$_{5}$(-d^{r})	see di-R
(nam--)ku$_{5}$(-d^{r})	see nam-R
(nam-érim--)ku$_{5}$(-d^{r})	see nam-érim--R
(še-gur$_{10}$--)ku$_{5}$(-d^{r})	see še-gur$_{10}$--R
(umbin--)ku$_{5}$(-d^{r})	see umbin--R
kur 1. (*šadûm*)	mountain; mountain range
2. (*mātum*)	land
kúr (*nakārum*)	to change
kuš (*maškum*)	skin (41 i 5)
kuš$_{7}$ (*kizûm*)	groom (see A. Cavigneaux, N.A.B.U. 1992/103)

lá 1. (*šaqālum*)	to weigh; to pay; to bear (in gu-za-lá)
2. (*maṭi*)	minus
(izi--)lá	see izi--lá
laḫ$_5$ (DU.DU; see DU)	to bring (used for a plural object)
(má-)laḫ$_5$	see má-R
límmu (*erbe*)	four
lu (*balālum*)	to mix
lú (*awīlum*)	person; man
lú-bàppir (*sirāšûm*)	brewer (for a possible reading of the variant LU$_2$.ŠIM / LU$_2$.ŠIMxG̃AR as ^{lú}lunga see P. Steinkeller, FAOS 17, 291)
lú-inim-ma (*šībum*)	witness (see S. Oh'e, ASJ 1 [1979] 69-84; I.J. Gelb et alii, OIP 104, 234)
lú-ki-inim-ma (*šībum*)	witness (see S. Oh'e, ASJ 1 [1979] 69-84; I.J. Gelb et alii, OIP 104, 233f.)
lú-má-gur$_8$	boat captain
lú-níg̃-tuku (cf. *rāšûm*)	debtor (lit.: a person who has something)
(nam-)lú-(inim-ma)	see nam-R-inim-ma
lugal 1. (*šarrum*)	king
2. (*bēlum*)	master; owner
(mu-)lugal	see mu-R
(mu-)lugal--(pà(-d))	see mu-R--pà(-d)
(nam-)lugal	see nam-R
(kù-)luḫ	see kù-R
(šu-)luḫ	see šu-R

ma-na (*manûm*)	mina (a unit of weight, ca. 500 gr.; see M. Powell, RlA 7, 510 § V.5)
má (*eleppum*)	ship
má-gíd	(the one) who tows the barge (full of first fruits to Enlil at Nippur; epithet of Gudea in 24 i 9)
má-gur$_8$ (*makurrum*)	cargo boat
(lú-)má-(gur$_8$)	see lú-R-gur$_8$
má-laḫ$_5$ (*malāḫum*)	sailor
maḫ (*ṣīrum*)	exalted; high
(sukkal-)maḫ	see sukkal-R
máš 1. (*lalûm; urīṣum*)	kid; he-goat
2. (*ṣibtum*)	produce; interest
maškim (*rābiṣum*)	commissioner (see D.O. Edzard/F.A.M. Wiggermann, RlA 7, 449ff.)

me 1. (*bašûm*)	to be
2. (*mû; parṣum*)	divine power that makes the institutions of heaven and earth function (see G. Farber-Flügge, RlA 7, 610ff.)
me-li$_9$(-m) (*melemmum*)	terrifying glance (literally: shining divine power)
mí (*sinništum*)	woman
(dumu-)mí	see dumu-R
(é-)mí	see é-R
(níĝ-)mí-(ús-sá)	see níĝ-R-ús-sá
min (*šina*)	two
mu 1. (*šumum*)	name
2. (*šattum*)	year
mu-...-a(k)-šè	because (in a nominalized sentence)
mu-lugal	see mu-lugal--pà(d)
mu-lugal--pà(-d)	to swear by the king, lit.: "to call the king's name", corresponding to the Akkadian *nīš šarrim zakārum* "to pronounce the king's life"; mu-lugal in 37:4 is an abbreviation for mu-lugal--pà
mu--pà(-d) ((*šumam*) *zakārum*)	to choose (lit.: to name (someone); said about the ruler chosen by the divinity)
mu-sar-ra (*mus/šarû*)	(royal) inscription
mu-šè--sa$_4$	to name; to give as name
mu-ús-sa (*šanītum šattum*)	the following year
mu-x	year-x (indicates a date according to a notable event that took place during the year)
mú (*waṣûm* Š)	to make grow
mul (*nabāṭum* G, Š)	to (let) shine
mun-du	morning offering (see J. Bauer AWL, 411 ad I 1; CAD M/II, 202 f, disc. section; L. Milano, RlA 8, 25 sub 3)
munus (*sinništum*)	woman
murgu-...-ta	after; for the reading murgu (= LUM) see E. Sollberger, AOAT 25, 440, note 15
mušen 1. (*iṣṣūrum*)	bird
2.	determinative for birds
na ([in alam/n-na(-ni-šè)] *abnum*)	stone (22 iii 2; 23 iii 16, iv 17; 26 ii 7); na is the original graph for the word 'stone' (usually written na$_4$), see P. Steinkeller, BiOr 52 (1995) 707
na-gada (*nāqidum*)	herdsman (loan from the Akkadian)
na-rú-a (*narûm*)	stele (lit.: 'set up, erected stone')
(ma-)na	see ma-R

na$_4$ 1. (*abnum*)	stone
2.	determinative for minerals and stones
nagar (*nagārum*)	carpenter
nam-	element used to form abstractions, such as in English -hood, -ship, and -scape
nam-érim (*māmītum*)	assertory oath
nam-érim--ku$_5$(-d^r)	to take the assertory oath
nam-érin	assertory oath (variant writing of nam-érim; see A. Falkenstein, NG 1, 64, note 2)
nam--ku$_5$(-d^r) (*nazārum*)	to curse
nam-lú-inim-ma (*šībūtum*)	the act of witnessing
nam-lugal (*šarrūtum*)	kingship
nam-nin (*bēlūtum*)	rulership; position of supreme power
nam-nir-g̃ál (*muttallūtu*)	distinction; superiority
nam-šita	prayer (29:24; see H. Behrens/H. Steible, FAOS 6, 250f.)
nam-tar (*šīmtum*)	destiny
nam--tar (*šiāmum*)	to decree a destiny
nam-ti(-l) (*balāṭum*)	life
nar (*nārum*)	musician
ne-ḫa (*nēḫtum*)	rest (loan from the Akkadian)
NE.NE-g̃ar	the fifth month in the Ur III calendar. Its Babylonian equivalent was the month of *abum* (see G.J. Selz, N.A.B.U. 1989/38; M. Cohen, Cultic Calendars, 100-104)
ní (*puluḫtum*)	awe, Ehrfurcht, Scheu
ní--tuku 1. (*palāḫum*)	to experience awe or fear
2. (*na'dum*)	awesome (cf. M.-J. Seux, Épithètes royales, 430f.)
ní--te(-g̃) (*palāḫum*)	to fear; to respect
níg̃ (*ša*)	a thing; something; a matter
níg̃-ak-ak (*epištum*)	deed; activity
níg̃-gu$_7$-a (*ukultum*)	consumption; food consumed
níg̃-gur$_{11}$ (*makkūrum*)	possession; property
níg̃-mí-ús-sa (*te/irḫatum*)	wedding gift (see C. Wilcke, Familiengründung, 252ff.; P. Steinkeller/J.N. Postgate, MC 4, 37f.)
níg̃-sám (*šīmum*)	price (see P. Steinkeller, FAOS 17, 153ff.)
(lú-)níg̃-(tuku)	see lú-R-tuku
níg̃-ú-rum (*makkūrum*)	possession; acquisition
níg̃-ul (*ša ṣiātim*)	what is fit for the cult (literally: what is primordial; for the reading ul rather than du$_7$ see Ur-Nammu 26 ii 1 in H. Steible, FAOS 9/2, 124f.)

níĝin 1. (*lawûm*)	to surround
2. (*saḫārum*)	to turn around; to go around; the *marû*-form NIĜIN$_2$.NIĜIN$_2$ (39:24) is most likely to be read ni$_{10}$-ni$_{10}$ (*ne/inni, see J. Krecher, Studies Matouš II, 53; 71, note 80; AOAT 240, 162)
(šu-)níĝin	see šu-R
niĝir (*nagīrum*)	herald
nin (*bēltum*)	lady
(nam-)nin	see nam-R
ninnu (*ḫam/nšā*)	fifty
(nam-)nir-ĝál	see nam-R
nita (*zikarum*)	male; manly
(saĝ-)nita	see saĝ-R
(udu-)nita	see udu-R
nu-bànda (*laputtûm*)	inspector; overseer; captain (see D.O. Edzard, ZANF 21 (1963) 91ff.; P. Attinger, ÉLS, 156f.)
nu-kiri$_6$(-k) (*nukarippum*)	gardener (for the etymology of the Akkadian *nukaribb/ppum* see M. Krebernik, BFE, 330)
(en-)nu-(uĝ$_5$)	see en-R-uĝ$_5$
(igi-)nu-(du$_8$)	see igi-R-du$_8$
numun (*zērum*)	seed
nun 1. (*rubûm*)	prince
2. (*rabûm*)	great; princely

pa--è (*wapûm* Š)	to let shine
pà(-d) (*nabûm*)	to call; to name
(mu-lugal--)pà(-d)	see mu-lugal--R
(mu--)pà(-d)	see mu--R
(šà(-ge)--)pà(-d)	see šà(-ge)--R
pa$_5$ (*palgum*)	ditch; canal
(ĝi$_6$-)par$_4$	see ĝi$_6$-R
pú (*būrtum*)	fountain

(du-)**rí**	see du-R
(šu-)rí	see šu-R
(saĝ--)rig$_7$	see saĝ--R
(a--)ru	see a--R
ru(-g)	to receive; to bring back (see G.J. Selz, ASJ 17 [1995] 274, note 103)
rú [*d^{r}u, see dù)] (*banûm*)	to raise up; to set up
(na-)rú-(a)	see na-R-a

(ú-)rum	see ú-R
sa (*riksum*)	bundle
sá-du$_{11}$ (*šattukkum*)	regular offering
sá--du$_{11}$-du$_{11}$	to provide regular offerings
sá-g̃ar (*mālikum*)	adviser; counsellor
(g̃^{iš}gag-si-)sá	see g̃^{iš}gag-si-R
(si--)sá-sá	see si--R-R
(mu-šè--)sa$_4$	see mu-šè--R (sa$_4$ is a conventional reading; in OB texts it should be read še$_{21}$)
sa$_6$(-g) 1. (*damqum*)	good
2. (*ṭābum*)	beautiful; fruitful
sa$_{10}$(-sa$_{10}$) (*šâmum*)	to buy
sag̃ 1. (*rēšum*)	head; an architectural feature
2. (*rēštum*)	first-class
3. (*rēštûm*)	first; first-class
sag̃-dub	regular worker (see G.J. Selz, FAOS 15/2, 230f.); the meaning of sag̃-dub in 36:3 remains doubtful, see A. Falkenstein, NG 2, 213, note to 3
sag̃-èn-tar (*pāqidum*)	overseer; guardian
sag̃--íl (*rēšam ullûm*)	to raise up; lit.: to lift the 'head' (of a wall or temple); 28:13-14; 29:30
sag̃-nita (*rēšum*)	(grown) man (see P. Steinkeller, FAOS 17, 130ff.)
sag̃--rig$_7$ (*šarākum*)	to donate (sag̃/sa$_{12}$--rig$_7$ may be a loan from the Akkadian *šarākum*)
sag̃-šu$_4$ (*kubšum*)	cap (see H. Waetzoldt, RlA 6, 200f.)
sag̃-ús (*rēšam kullum*)	to be available; to care for something's maintenance (cf. M.-J. Seux, Épithètes royales, 440)
(ḫur-)sag̃	see ḫur-R
(ur-)sag̃	see ur-R
sag̃g̃a (*šangûm*)	temple-administrator
sagi (*šāqûm*)	cup-bearer (loan from the Akkadian; see J.-J. Glassner, RlA 8, 420-422)
saḫar (*eperum*)	dust; earth
sar 1. (*šaṭārum*)	to write
2. (*mus/šarum*)	a surface measure: 1 s/šar = 60 gig̃$_4$ = 1/100 *ikûm* (see RlA 7, 479 § II.5)
(mu-)sar-(ra)	see mu-R-ra
sè(-g/k) (*šakānum*)	to set (according to J. Krecher, AOAT 240, 195 the verbal roots sè(-g) and sè(-k) must be distinguished)

(àga-kár--)sè(-g)	see àga-kár--R
si-(si(-g)) (*malûm* D)	to fill in
(asila$_x$--)si-si	see asila$_x$--R-R
si-sá (*išarum*)	right; legal
si--sá-sá (*ešērum* Š; Št)	to get ready (24 iii 2); to yoke (25 iii 12-13)
(^{ĝiš}gag-)si-(sá)	see ^{ĝiš}gag-R-sá
sig$_4$ (*libittum*)	unbaked brick
sig$_4$-báḫar(-ra) (cf. *agurrum*)	baked(?)/potter's(?) brick; possibly to be read sig$_4$(/šeg$_{12}$)-alur$_x$-ra, see P. Steinkeller, JNES 46 (1987) 59; JNES 52 (1993) 145
(kas-)sig$_{15}$	see kas-R (is sig$_{15}$ a syllabic writing of sig$_{17}$ (GI) "light colored"?)
siki (*šīpātum*)	wool
(udu-)siki	see udu-R
sikil (*ellum*)	pure; virginal
sìla (*qûm*)	a measure of capacity; liter-vessel; in Pre-Sargonic Lagaš as well as in the standard Akkad-Old Babylonian system 1 sìla equals approximately 1 liter (see M. Powell, RlA 7, 497 § IV.4-5)
sila$_4$ (*puḫādum*)	lamb
sipa(-d) (*rē'ûm*)	shepherd
(é-TAR-)sír-(sír)	see *Sacred Buildings*
(pa$_5$-)sír-(ra)	see *Place Names*
su (*zumrum; šīrum* [text 28])	body; flesh (28:7, 24); as for 39:13 su/kuš = *zumrum/maškum* must be taken into consideration, cf. A. Cavigneaux/F. Al-Rawi, ZA 83 [1993] 202-205
sù-sù(-g)	to satisfy$^{?}$ (34 v 1; this translation is based on the context; sù-sù(-g), literally "to make empty" remains difficult)
su$_{13}$(-d^{r}) (*arākum* G, D)	to be long; to lenghten; to last
suḫuš (*išdum*)	foundation
sukkal (*šukkallum*)	courier; a high-ranking official (the reading sukkal is conventional; in OB and Pre-OB sources sugal$_7$ is preferable)
sukkal-maḫ (*sukkalmaḫḫu*)	prime-minister
sur	the meaning of sur in 39:21 remains uncertain

ša	element used in fractions
šà(-g) (*libbum*)	content; interior
šà(-ge--)pà(-d)	to choose (lit.: to call in the heart)
šà-bi-ta	from it (lit.: from its inside)

(zi-)šà-(g̃ál)	see zi-R-g̃ál
^{dug}šab (*šappum*)	pot; vessel
(ka-)šakan	see ka-R (the reading šakan/šagan for $ŠU_4.GAN_4$ is conventional)
šár(-šár) (*dešûm* D)	to make abundant
še (*še'um*)	grain; barley
še-ga (*migrum*)	favorite (cf. M.-J. Seux, Épithètes royales, 448ff.)
še-gur_{10}-ku_5(-d^r) (*eṣēdum*)	The twelfth month in the Ur III calendar. Its Babylonian equivalent was the month of *a(d)daru*. The Sumerian means *eṣēdum* "to harvest" (see M. Cohen, Cultic Calendars, 119-124). The reading gur_{10} is not certain, see M. Civil, FI, 170f.; J. Bauer, JAOS 115 [1995] 294
(DUB.)ŠEN	see DUB.R
šeš (*aḫum*)	brother (for a reading ses instead of šeš see J. Bauer, AoN 1985, 2, n. 21)
šim 1. (*rīqum*)	scent; fragrance
2.	fragrant
3.	determinative for perfumes
(nam-)šita	see nam-R
šitim (*itinnum*)	house builder
šu (*qātum*)	hand; control
šu--ba(-d^r/r) (*wuššurum*)	to release (see J. Krecher, Kutscher Memorial Vol., 111ff.)
šu--du_7-du_7 (*šuklulum*)	to complete; to finish
($giri_{17}$-)šu--(g̃ál)	see $giri_{17}$-R--g̃ál
šu--gi_4	to lead back; to bring back; to give back
šu--tag (*za'ānum* D)	to decorate; to adorn
šu--ti (*leqûm*)	to receive
šu--ùr (*pašāṭum*)	to erase (an inscription; lit.: to flatten the hand [on something])
šu-dag̃al--du_{11}	to supply with abundantly
šu-du_8-a--DU(de_6/túm)	to act as guarantor for (see J. Marzahn/H. Neumann, AoF 22 [1995] 115, ad II 1')
šu-gibil-gibil--ak	to renew
šu-luḫ (*šuluḫḫum*)	purification ritual (cf. G. Farber-Flügge, St.Pohl 10, 191ff.)
šu-níg̃in (*napḫarum*)	total
šu-rí (*mišlānu*)	half (see J. Friberg, RlA 7, 536 § 3.1; G.J. Selz, ASJ 17 [1995] 274)
šu-tag--du_{11} (*za'ānum* D)	to sprinkle (in 23 iii 8-10 and 25 iii 3-5 it is said about oil (ì) and fine scent (ir-nun))
(sag̃-)$šu_4$	see sag̃-R

(g̃á-^{giš}ù-)šub-(ba)	see g̃á-^{giš}ù-R-ba
šùba (cf. *namrum*)	shining (like the colour of the šùba-stone [agate?]; for the variant readings /š/suba/, /subi/ see Å. Sjöberg, JCS 40 [1988] 172f., note 6)
šudul (*nīrum*)	yoke (the reading šudul for $ŠU_4.DUL_4$ is conventional)
šúm (*nadānum*)	to give; to hand over; to lend
(zà--)šuš	see zà-R
šušana (*šuššān*)	one third
(ki-...-)ta	see ki-...-R
(murgu-...-)ta	see murgu-...-R
(g̃iš--)tag	see g̃iš--R
(šu--)tag	see šu--R
(šu-)tag--(du_{11})	see šu-R--du_{11}
(g̃ál--)$taka_4$	see g̃ál--R
(kù-dam-)$taka_4$	see kù-dam-R
(nam--)tar	see nam--R
(sag̃-èn-)tar	see sag̃-èn-R
(é-)TAR-(sír-sír)	see *Sacred Buildings*
(ní--)te(-g̃)	see ní--R
temen (*temmēnum*)	foundation peg (see S. Dunham, RA 80 [1986] 31-64)
ti(-l) (*balāṭum*)	life (the form a-ba-ti-la-da "so long as he lives" is difficult to explain. According to PSD A/I, 47, 5. s.v. a-ba, it is sandhi writing. A. Falkenstein, NG 3, 166 s.v. ti(l) suggests that it means u_4 ba-ti-la-da)
(g̃iš-kíg̃-)ti	see g̃iš-kíg̃-R
(nam-)ti	see nam-R
(šu-)ti	see šu--R
til (*gamārum*)	to destroy; to exterminate
(di-)til-(la)	see di-R-la
tir (*qištum*)	forest; grove (PEa 457: te-er)
tu(-d) (*walādum*)	to give birth; to make (a statue 21 iii 9-10; 22 iii 2-3); the traditional reading tu(-d) is retained here since PEa 684-685 notes tu-ú [= *marû*?] as well as du-ú [= *ḫamṭu*?]; see J. Krecher, AOAT 240, 160f.
túg (*ṣubātum*)	garment; clothing
tuku 1. (*išûm*)	to have; with the infix /-da-/: to have a claim against somebody (30:5, 8)
2. (*aḫāzum*)	to marry

(lú-níĝ-)tuku	see lú-níĝ-R
(ní-)tuku	see ní-R
tukumbi (*šumma*)	if; in case
túm	see DU
(^{d}ĝá-)tùm-(du$_{10}$(-g))	see *Divine Names*
tuš (*wašābum* G, Š)	to cause to dwell; to settle (for the plural form of this verb see durun$_{x}$)
(ki-)tuš	see ki-R
ú (*šammum*)	grass; a plant
ú-a (*zāninum*)	provider; supplier (cf. M.-J. Seux, Épithètes royales, 456ff.)
ú-rum	possession (see G.J. Selz, FAOS 15/2, 110f.)
ú-durun$_{x}$(DUR$_{2}$.DUR$_{2}$)-na	brushwood(?); hay(?); for a discussion of this term (oven-grass?) see G.J. Selz, FAOS 15/2, 320f.
(^{d}ba-)U$_{2}$	see *Divine Names*
ù--ku$_{4}$ (*ṣalālum*)	to sleep; to rest (see (ù--)ku$_{4}$)
(ĝá-)^{ĝiš}ù-šub-ba	see ĝá-R
u$_{4}$ (*ūmum*)	day
u$_{4}$-...(-a) (*inu*)	when
u$_{4}$-ba (*ina ūmīšu*)	at that time; then
u$_{4}$-bi-ta	the past (literally: from those days)
u$_{4}$-šú-uš-e (*ūmišam*)	daily; day by day
u$_{4}$-ul-lí-a-ta (*ištu ūm ṣiātim*)	from long ago (for the meaning of ul and /i/ in this expression see J. van Dijk, AcOr 28 [1964] 33)
u$_{8}$ (*laḫrum*)	ewe
u$_{18}$-ru (*ṣīrum; elûm*)	exalted; high (see M.-C. Ludwig, SANTAG 2, 107ff.)
ub (*tubqum*)	corner; a small room
(an-)ub-(da)	see an-R-da
ud$_{5}$ [*uzd] (*enzum*)	goat (see A. Cavigneaux, SAZ, 55f.; J. Bauer, AoN 1987, 2, n. 31; for the proposed reading /uzud/ see G. Selz, WO 26 [1995] 196)
udu (*immerum*)	sheep
udu-nita (*immerum*)	ram
udu-siki	wool-bearing sheep
ùĝ (*nišū*)	people; population
(en-nu-)uĝ$_{5}$	see en-nu-R
ugu (*eli*)	on; over (the reading ugu for U.GU$_{3}$ is conventional)
ugula (*waklum*)	chief; overseer (loan from the Akkadian)
ul (cf. *ullûm*)	distant (in time, either past or future)

(níĝ-)ul	see níĝ-R
(u$_4$-)ul-(lí-a-ta)	see u$_4$-R-lí-a-ta
umbin--ku$_5$(-d^r) (*gullubum*)	to shave; to shear (literally: to pluck with the fingernail)
umuš (*ṭēmum*)	decision; understanding (29 i 6)
unken (*puḫrum*)	assembly (<*ùĝ-kíĝ, lit.: seeking (= consulting) the people)
unu$_6$ (*mūšabum*; *šubtum*; *mākālum*)	living room; dining room? (where the gods received their food offerings); sanctuary (cf. A. Falkenstein, OrNS 35 [1966] 239ff.; D. Charpin, clergé, 337ff.)
ur (*kalbum*)	dog; for the meaning of ur in Personal Names like ur-^{d}DN see R. Di Vito, StPohl SM 16, 116ff.; for Akkadian PN's containing the element *kalbum* see CAD K, 72 i)
ur-saĝ (*qarrādum*)	hero
(šu--)ùr	see šu--R
úrdu(-d) (*wardum*)	slave; servant; subordinate
uri (*akkadûm*)	Akkadian
(ki-)uri	see ki-R
urin (*urinnum*)	standard
uru$_{12}$	the reading uru$_{12}$ expresses the verbal root ùr (see šu--ùr) plus the verbal ending -e
uru$_{16}$(-n) (*dannum*; *naklum*)	strong; clever (see M. Civil, Studies Sjöberg, 55)
ús 1. (*redûm*)	to (make) follow
2. (*emēdum*)	to border; when said about ships, to dock
(saĝ-)ús	see saĝ-R
(mu-)ús-(sa)	see mu-R-sa
(níĝ-mí-)ús-(sa)	see níĝ-mí-R-sa
uš (*uššum*)	foundation; pit(?)
(àga-)ús	see àga-R
ušumgal (*ušumgallum*)	dragon (lit.: big snake)
utul (*utullum*)	herdsman (<*udu+lu, pasturing sheep)
(^{d}šul-)utul$_{12}$	see *Divine Names*

za-gìn (*uqnûm*)	lapis-lazuli
(^{ĝiš}gu-)za	see ^{ĝiš}gu-R
zà(-g)--šuš (cf. *šimtum*)	to brand; to mark (see D. Foxvog, ZA 85 [1995] 1ff.)

zal 1. (*šutebrûm*)	to pass
2. (*nasāḫum*)	when said about dating, u_4-x zal-la means "on the xth day"
zi(-d) (*kīnum*)	true; lawful, right; legitimate; legitimating
zi-g̃ál-la (*šiknat napištim*)	living being
zi-šà-g̃ál (*zišagallu*)	divine encouragement; inspiration (see J. Klein, ThŠH, 151 ad 52)
zi(-r) (*pasāsum* D)	to destroy; to annihilate
-zu (*-ka/-ki*)	your
(gal-)zu	see gal-R
(a-ra-)zu	see a-ra-R
zú--kéš (cf. *kaṣārum; rakāsum*)	to oblige; for zú--kéš(-d^r [*kešed^r / kšed^r]) see A. Cavigneaux/F. Al-Rawi, ZA 85 (1995) 36ff.

AKKADIAN

ilum (dig̃ir)	(the) god
-ma	and
mālikum (ad-gi_4-gi_4)	counselor; adviser
puḫrum (unken)	assembly; council
rīmum	gift
šemûm (g̃iš--tuku)	to hear
šu (cf. lú)	the one who belongs to (in proper names of the *šu*-DN type)
u (-bi-da)	and
ummum (ama)	mother

AMORITE

ḫammu(m) [*'ammu(m)*]	paternal uncle ("grandfather" according to J.M. Durand, CRRA 38 [1992] 120, note 174)
rāpi'u(m)	healer

DIVINE NAMES

Each name is accompanied by:

1) *Its etymology;* 2) *The chief cult place;* 3) *The god's chief features.*

^{d}**ama-ušumgal-an-na**: 1) "'Lord-dragon' of Heaven" (see G.J. Selz, UGASL, 21f.); 3) Associated with Lugaluru(b) in Pre-Sargonic Lagaš; eventually assimilated to Dumuzi.

an: 1) "Heaven"; 2) Uruk; 3) Personification of heaven; nominal head of the Sumerian pantheon.

^{d}**anzu**(-d)^{mušen} (for the latest study of this name see B. Alster, RA 85 [1991] 1ff.); 3) Personification of the storm-cloud, represented as a white eagle. Anzu stole the tablet of destiny from Enlil, but Niĝirsu conquered him, returned the tablet to Enlil, and thus became his ur-saĝ-kala-ga.

^{d}**ba-U$_2$**: 2) Goddess of Iriku(-g) in Lagaš (see G.J. Selz, UGASL, 26ff.); 3) Vegetation goddess; Niĝirsu's wife.

^{d}**da-gan**: 2) The region of Mari; 3) The West-Semitic storm-god, originally a chtonic god (cf. D.R. Frayne, BCSMS 25 [1993] 40 with note 31-41).

^{d}**da-mu**: 3) A god of healing; one of the disappearing and dying gods whose sister goes to search for him.

^{d}**dumu-zi**(-d): 1) "'True Child'" (cf. Th. Jacobsen, JQR 76 [1985] 41-45); 2) God of Badtibira; 3) There are two traditions: one about Dumuzi the fisherman and one about Dumuzi the sheperd. The fisherman is from Ku'ara, the shepherd is from Badtibira. The shepherd is Inanna's "husband" whom she sends to the underworld to substitute her. He is the archetypal disappearing and dying god.

^{d}**dumu-zi-abzu**: 1) "'True Child' of the Abyss"; 2) Kinuniršа; 3) This divinity was generally regarded as female. At Eridu, however, it was considered male and formed part of Enki's entourage.

^{d}**en-ki**(-g/-k): 1) "Lord of the Earth"; 2) Eridu; 3) The crafty god of magic and wisdom; the helper of mankind. This divinity is to be distinguished from **en-ki** "Lord Earth", one of the gods who existed before the separation of heaven and earth.

^{d}**en-líl**: 1) "Lord Breeze" is a popular etymology. What *e/illil really means is unknown. 2) Nippur; 3) The *de facto* head of the Sumerian pantheon.

^{d}**èr-ra**: 3) A Semitic warrior and plague god who is identified with underworld deities.

^{d}**eš$_{5}$-peš**: 2) Adab; 3) A divinity found in third-millenium god-lists from Fara and Abū-Ṣalabīkh, as well as Early-Dynastic and Early Sargonic mythological texts (see B. Alster/A. Westenholz, ASJ 16 [1994] 37).

^{d}**éštar**: 3) Save for the absence of the sacred marriage, she was the Semitic eqivalent of Inanna, with whom she was syncretized.

^{d}**g̃á-tùm-du$_{10}$**(-g): 2) Lagaš (see G.J. Selz, UGASL, 134ff.); 3) The mother-goddess at Lagaš; special protectress of Gudea.

^{d}**ig-alim**: 1) "Door of the Bison" (see G.J. Selz, UGASL, 144ff.); 2) Lagaš; 3) Šul-šagana's twin brother; the son of Ba'U and Ning̃irsu.

^{d}**inanna**: 1) "Lady of Heaven" is a popular etymology; 2) Uruk; 3) The planet Venus; the heavenly courtesan; a warrior goddess; a Vegetation goddess whose sacred marriage to Dumuzi, repeated every new-year's day, guaranteed Sumer's fertility. She was syncretized with the Semitic E/Ištar and was most commonly thought to be the daughter of Nanna-*Su'en*. As for her relationship to An, the god of the sky, see J. van Dijk, Studies Borger, 9-11; 30.

^{d}**iškur**: 2) Karkara; 3) The storm god.

^{d}**ištaran**: 2) Dēr; 3) A god connected with judgement.

^{d}**lugal-uru$_{x}$(URUxKAR$_{2}$)**^{ki}(-b): 1) "King of Uru(b)" (see G.J. Selz, UGASL, 163ff.); 2) Uru(b); 3) Syncretism identified him with Inanna's husband Dumuzi.

^{d}**marduk**: 1) The interpretation and milieu of the name *Marud/tuk (cf. the biblical Merōdaḫ) remain unclear. Certainly it is not, as popular etymology would have it, "calf of the sun god"; 2) Babylon; 3) Chief god of Babylon and, in the first millenium, head of the whole pantheon because of his victory over Tiamat.

^{d}**nammu/a**: 3) In the cosmogony of Eridu, the goddess who personified the primordial waters. For a reading namma rather than nammu see M. Civil, OrNS 54 (1985) 27, note 1.

^{d}**nanna**: 2) Ur; 3) The Sumerian moon-god. His en-priestess lived in the Gipar at the Karzida in Ur and was one of the major personages in Sumerian religion. The god was identified with *Su'en/Sîn*, the Semitic moon-god.

^{d}**nanše**: 2) Sirara / Nina (see G.J. Selz, UGASL, 181ff.); 3) Ningirsu's sister; interpreter of dreams; protectress of birds and fish; goddess of "social justice".

^{d}**nin-a-zu**: 1) "Lord Physician"; 2) Enegi; 3) An underworld healing-god; Ninĝišzida's father.

^{d}**nin-dar**: 2) Ki'eš; 3) Nanše's husband. The reading dar (not gùn) in the second part of the name is discussed by M. Civil, Studies Sjöberg, 50.

^{d}**nin-ĝír-su**: 1) "Lord of Ĝirsu" (see G.J. Selz, UGASL, 218ff.); 2) Ĝirsu; 3) Ba'U's husband; he became Enlil's hero when he recovered the tablet of destiny that Anzu had stolen.

^{d}**nin-ĝiš-zi-da**: 1) "Lord of the True Tree"; 2) Ĝišbanda; 3) Ninazu's son; an underworld snake-god; Gudea's patron god. The latter seemingly introduced him into the Lagaš pantheon to justify his own assumption of power.

^{d}**nin-ḫur-saĝ**: 1) "Lady of the Mountain-Range"; 2) Keši; 3) The mother-goddess. Her name indicates where she appears. She is the creator of gods and men.

^{d}**nin-líl**: 1) "Lady Breeze" (popular etymology analogous to ^{d}en-líl "lord breeze"); 2) Nippur; 3) Enlil's wife.

^{d}**nin-MAR.KI**: 1) "Lady of Marg/ki"(?; see P. Attinger, N.A.B.U. 1995/33); 2) Guabba; 3) Nanše's daughter.

^{d}**nin-šubur**: 1) "Lord / Lady of (the land of) Šubur/Subar(?)"; 2) Akkil; 3) When male, An's sukkal; when female, Inanna's sukkal.

^{d}**nin-te-ug$_{5}$-ga**: 1) By popular etymology "Lady who Keeps the Dying Alive"; cf. Marduk's epithet *muballiṭ mīti*; 3) A goddess of healing.

^{d}**nu-muš-da**: 2) Kazallu.

^{d}**nun-gal**: 1) "Great Nobility"; 2) Nippur; 3) A goddess connected with justice and judgement, especially the judicial ordeal.

^{d}**NUNUZ.KAD$_{4}$^{mušen}**: 3) The determinative mušen shows that the divinity is a bird (see G. Pettinato, MEE 3, 112:79; 117, l. 79).

^{d}**su'en** › ^{d}**sîn**: 1) The original meaning of this name is uncertain (see M. Krebernik, RlA 8, 362f.). According to D.R. Frayne, BCSMS 25 (1993) 40, it might go back to a Proto-Indo-European root; 2) Ur; 3) The Semitic moon-god identified with Nanna, the Sumerian moon-god.

^{d}**šára**: 2) Umma; 3) Inanna's son; her manicurist and hair-dresser.

^{d}**šul-šà-ga-na** 1) "The Lad of his (Nin̄girsu's) Heart" (see G.J. Selz, UGASL, 277ff.); 2) Lagaš; 3) Igalim's twin brother; the son of Ba'U and Nin̄girsu.

^{d}**šul-utul**$_{12}$ 1) "The Lad who Pastures Sheep" (see G.J. Selz, UGASL, 279ff.); 2) Lagaš; 3) Dynastic god of the rulers of Lagaš from Urnanše to Enmetena.

^{d}**utu**: 1) "Sun"; 2) Sippar; 3) The sun god.

For further reading see:

Black, J. - Green, A., Gods, Demons and Symbols of Ancient Mesopotamia. An Illustrated Dictionary (London 1992).
Edzard, D.O., in H.W. Haussig, Wörterbuch der Mythologie, Band I (Stuttgart 1965) 19-139.
Leick, G., A Dictionary of Ancient Near Eastern Mythology (London/New York 1991).
Selz, G.J., Untersuchungen zur Götterwelt des altsumerischen Stadtstaates von Lagaš (Occasional Publications of the Samuel Noah Kramer Fund 13, Philadelphia 1995).
The relevant articles in the Reallexikon der Assyriologie (RlA).
For the Lagaš pantheon of the Gudea period: the relevant articles in A. Falkenstein, Die Inschriften Gudeas von Lagaš. I. Einleitung (AnOr 30, Rome 1966).

PERSONAL NAMES

(Parentheses indicate the text in which the name appears)

a-ba-^{d}utu-gim (30:4)
a-kur-gal (15 i 4; 16 ii 1). A ruler of Pre-Sargonic Lagaš.
á-lu$_5$-lu$_5$ (38:26)
ad-da-šu-sikil (34 vi 1)
ama-iri (35:8)
^{d}amar-^{d}*su'en* (27:4, 19, 25). A ruler of Ur in the Ur III period.
ba-ši-šà-ra-gi (32:3)
bára-nam-tar-ra (34 iv 1). The wife of Lugalanda, a Pre-Sargonic ruler of Lagaš.
BU-KA (36:9)
diğir-a-ğu$_{10}$ (33 iv 2)
du-du (38:4, 6, 7, 12, 16, 18, 20, 22, 28, 34, 40, 43)
du-du-ú (36:12)
é-an-na-tum (16 i 1; iii 9). A ruler of Pre-sargonic Lagaš.
é-me-li$_9$-sù (34 iii 3)
en-an-na-túm (I) (14:13; 15 i 1; 20:10; 21 i 10)
en-an-na-túm (II) (19:3, 16)
en-ig-gal (34 v 4; 40 ii 1; 42 iii 2; 44 ii 4)
^{d}en-líl-lá-an-zu (36:10)
en-lú (34 vi 6)
en-šu (34 v 6)
en-te:me-na [= en-me-te-na] (11:1; 13:3; 8; 14:3; 19:10; 20:3; 20; 31; 21 i 3; iii 8:11; iv 2, 7; vi 2). For the reading of this name see H. Steible, FAOS 5/2, 106 (1).
^{d}*èr-ra-ma-lik* (39:3)
^{d}*éštar-um-mi* (39:1)
gan-ki (34 ii 5)
géme-^{d}ig-alim (37:15)
géme-^{d}nun-gal (31:4)
géme-ti-ra-áš (38:36)
gi-zi (38 ii 13)
ğišgal-si (34 ii 6)
gu-NI-DU (12 i 4). The father(?) of ur-^{d}nanše, a ruler of Pre-Sargonic Lagaš.
gù-dé-a (2:3; 4:3; 5:3; 6:4; 7:4; 8:4; 9:4; 10:6; 22 r. sh. 1; i 5; iii 7; 23 i 2; ii 4, 14; iii 18; 24 r. sh. 1; i 5; iv 4; v 5; 25 r. sh. 1; i 3; ii 6; 26 i 7; iii 4). A ruler of Lagaš whose dating is uncertain. Perhaps he should be placed in the period that goes from the Guteans to the beginning of Ur III.
ḫa-am-mu-ra-pí (28:1, 21, 33). A ruler of Babylon in the Old-Babylonian period.
ì-lí-A.ZU (39:2)
ì-lí-DIĞIR^{lum} (36:7)

in-na-sa$_6$-ga (38:3, 8, 10, 13, 16, 21, 34, 40)
inim-lugal (37:13)
iri-KA-gi-na (17:3; 18 i 3; iv 5). A ruler of Pre-Sargonic Lagaš; for the latest discussion of the reading of this name see P. Steinkeller, JAOS 115 (1995) 541-542.
IŠ (30:13)
^{d}*iš-me-*^{d}*da-gan*-zi-g̃u$_{10}$ (39:28)
ka$_5{}^{a}$ (36:13)
la-la (34 v 2; vii 2)
lú-^{d}da-mu (36:14)
lú-dig̃ir-ra (32:10; 37:21; 38:49)
lú-g̃u$_{10}$ (32:7)
lú-ib-gal (37:20)
lú-^{d}inanna (36:1)
lú-^{d}iškur (31:9)
lú-^{d}nin-šubur (36:15)
lú-sa$_6$-ga (36:2)
lú-^{d}šára (32:8; 37:9, 19; 38:48)
lugal-á-gur-ra (34 ii 1)
lugal-á-zi-da (31:3)
lugal-an-da (34 iv 2; 43 ii 3). A ruler of Pre-Sargonic Lagaš.
lugal-da (33 iii 3)
lugal-DUR$_2$ (30:11)
lugal-eden-né (34 i 1)
lugal-ḫé-g̃ál (31:10)
lugal-igi-ḫuš (37:8)
lugal-iti-da (36:17)
lugal-ki-gal-la (37:5)
lugal-níg̃-zu (35:1)
lugal-ra-mu-gi$_4$ (34 vi 8)
ma-gi-na (38 iii 12)
munus-kur-ra (43 i 2)
nam-ḫa-ni (36:8)
nam-maḫ (38:25)
^{d}nanše:ur, see ur-^{d}nanše
níg̃-gur$_{11}$ (35:9)
níg̃-ú-rum (37:2, 9, 11, 12, 16)
nin-a-na (38:15, 39)
nin-inim-zi-da (35:3)
ni-za (38:15, 32, 39)
pú-ta (31:10)
ri-im-^{d}*sîn* (29 i 13). A ruler of Larsa in the Old-Babylonian period.
sa$_6$-sa$_6$ (44 vii 1). The wife of IriKAgina, a ruler of Pre-Sargonic Lagaš.
sag̃-^{d}ba-U$_2$-tuku (38:38)

šà-šu-níĝin (32:2)
šeš-lú-du$_{10}$ (40 i 2)
šeš-sa$_{6}$-ga (44 vi 5)
šu-duran ([DUR$^{!}$.KIB] 31:5)
^{d}*šu*-^{d}*sîn* (32:12)
ti-ti (38:4)
ú-šè-ḫé-DU (32:2)
ur-ba-gára (38:47)
ur-^{d}ba-U$_{2}$ (37:8)
ur-du$_{6}$ (42 ii 1)
ur-^{d}dumu-zi (43 iii 3)
ur-é-mùš (33 i 3; 34 vi 3)
ur-é-ninnu (38:7)
ur-^{d}eš$_{5}$-peš (30:2)
ur-gu-la (38:24)
ur-^{d}ig-alim (32:7; 37:6)
ur-^{d}inanna (35:7)
ur-^{d}iškur (31:2, 7)
ur-^{d}ištaran (32:9; 37:18,22; 38:50)
ur-kèš^{ki} (30:6)
ur-ki (33 ii 4)
ur-^{d}nammu (1:3; 3:3)
ur-^{d}nanše 1) A ruler of Pre-Sargonic Lagaš (12 i 1 [written: ^{d}nanše:ur]; 21 i 14).
2) A party in a wedding contract (32:3).
ur-nìgin-ĝar (36:11)
ur-^{d}nin-MAR.KI (41 ii 2)
ur-^{d}‹nu-›muš-da (37:2)
ur-^{d}NUNUZ.KAD$_{4}$^{mušen} (38:47)
ur-^{d}*sîn* (31:8)
ur-zu$^{(!)}$ (35:4; 6)
úrdu-^{d}nanna (38:19)
utu-lú-ĝu$_{10}$ (34 iii 2)

For further information about these names see R.A. Di Vito, Studies in Third Millennium Sumerian and Akkadian Personal Names. The Designation and Conception of the Personal God. Studia Pohl: Series Maior 16 (Rome 1993).

PLACE NAMES

^{i7}buranun (*purattu*) [28:16]: The Euphrates (UD.KIB.NUN read as bar_6-ùl-nun seems to be syllabic writing).

dilmun^{ki}: The region between what today is Falaika and Baḫrain.

(^{i7})**duran** [31:5]: The river Diyāla. See D.O. Edzard, RGTC 1, 210. For the reading of d/tur(r)an (DUR.KIB) see MSL X, 26-27; K. Nashef, BaM 13 (1982) 120, note 15; 133f., note 72.

é-GUM.DUR$_2$(-ra) [38:2, 35]: Meaning and reading unknown.

elam^{ki}: The region in south-west Iran with Susa as its center. It and Lagaš were hereditary enemies.

eridu^{ki}(-g): A city in Sumer and the center of Enki's cult. The name seems to mean "Good City".

g̃ír-su^{ki}: An important settlement that was part of the city-state of Lagaš. Its god was Ning̃irsu.

gu-bi^{ki}(-n): The location of this land, mentioned in 25 iv 9 in the sequence Magan, Meluḫḫa, Gubi, and Dilmun, is uncertain. See D.T. Potts, N.A.B.U. 1996/65.

gú-eden-na: "The Border of the Steppe"; the boundary between Lagaš and Umma, object of constant war between the two states. See H.J. Nissen, AS 20, 34f.

IM.KA.šub$_5$(ZI.ZI.ŠE$_3$): A place mentioned in 21 v 2 whose reading is uncertain. See H. Steible / H. Behrens, FAOS 5/2, 109-110, note 15; J. Bauer, AoN 1987, 6, n. 39.

im-sag̃ (18 iii 9): While this may be the name of a place, the location of Enlil's temple é-ad-da, it could just as likely be the temple's epithet. It is discussed in H. Steible / H. Behrens, FAOS 5/2, 109f., note 15.

iri-kù(-g): "Holy City". A section of G̃irsu where the temple of Ba'U was located (see AnOr 30, 121; 141; for other early evidence about this toponym see V. Crawford, Iraq 36 [1974] 29ff.).

KA$_2$.DIG̃IR.RA^{ki}: "Gate of God". This sumerogram for the name of Babylon is a popular etymology based on the semitic *bāb ili*. For the likely genuine place-name *babilla see B. Kienast, Sumer 35 (1979) 246-248.

ká-sur-ra (24 iii 6): "Boundary Gate" where kar-za-gìn, "The Lapis-lazuli Quay" was located. But it is not clear exactly where ká-sur-ra was.

kar-nun (24 iii 4): "Princely Quay". Ba'U's magur-boat is connected with this place (24 iii 3).

kar-silim-ma (28:19): "Quay of Well-being"; located at Zimbir.

kar-za-gìn (24 iii 6): "Lapis-lazuli Quay" or "Pure Quay"; located at ká-sur-ra.

kar-zi-da (27:15): "The True Quay". At Ur, the location of the G̃ipar where Nanna's en-priestess lived.

ki-en-gi(-r) (*keg̃ir): "Native Land". The Sumerian name for their land (see C. Wilcke, CRRA 19 [1974] 202ff.; P. Steinkeller, HANE/S 5, 112, note 9; H. Steible, Ist.Mitt. 43 [1993] 25f.).

ki-lagaš^{ki} (29:17): The city-state of Lagaš, whose chief settlements where Lagaš, G̃irsu and Nina(-Sirara); see M. Yoshikawa, ASJ 7 [1985] 157ff.).

ki-uri: The Sumerian name for the land of Akkade. uri is the Sumerian rendering of the Semitic *war(i)* (see P. Steinkeller, HANE/S 5, 115f., note 18).

lagaš^{ki}: The settlement Lagaš in the state of the same name (see M. Yoshikawa, ASJ 7 [1985] 157ff.).

larsa^{ki}(-m): The Sumerian city of the sun-god. It ruled Sumer in Old-Babylonian times between the fall of Isin and the rise of Babylon.

má-gan^{ki}: A district corresponding to modern Oman; the source of precious metals, stone, and wood.

me-luḫ-ḫa^{ki}: In the third and early second millennium this was probably the area of the Mohenjo-Daro civilization.

nibru^{ki} (*nippuru*): Enlil's city, the religious center of Sumer.

nina^{ki}: A settlement in the state of Lagaš whose goddess was Nanše.

pa$_5$**-kù**(-g) [21 v 4]: "Pure canal"; located near Nina .

pa_5-sír-ra (21 ii 11): "The Sira Canal", where Enmetena built an abzu for Enki. See D.O. Edzard, RGTC 1, 136f.

si-ma-núm^{ki} (38:51): A city locted near modern Mardin in south-eastern Turkey; it was destroyed during *Šu-Sîn*'s third year.

su_{11}-lum (21 ii 7): The location of Nanše's temple é-engur-ra, "House of the Abyss" (see RGTC 1, 147).

sur-^{d}nanše (21 v 1): "Border of Nanše". Its location is unknown; see FAOS 5, 108, n.12. According to J. Cooper, SARI I, 64 n. 5 (ad La 5.17) "it is unclear if this is a personal or a geographical name".

šeš-g̃ar-ra (14:2): "Established by the Brother (Ning̃irsu)". This refers to Nanše's chapel in the Eninnu at G̃irsu. It remains uncertain whether in our text the phrase is the name of the temple é-šeš-g̃ar-ra or just Nanše's epithet.

šubur: Subartu, the land to the north of Mesopotamia; it seems to appear in the name of the divinity ^{d}nin-šubur (see Divine Names).

tir-kù(-g) (21 ii 15): "Pure 'Forest'". The location of Ninḫursag̃'s gi-gù-na that Enmetena built.

umma^{ki}: A Sumerian city, the hereditary enemy of Lagaš.

unug^{ki} (*uruk*): The city of An and Inanna.

uri$^{ki}_{2/5}$(-m): Nanna's city; Eannatum conquered it (16 ii 10). It became the capital of the Ur III dynasty that ruled Sumer and Akkad during the last century of the third millenium.

uru_x(URUxKAR$_2$)^{ki}(-b): A settlement in the state of Lagaš. In text 20 it is mentioned in connection with offerings to its god Lugaluru(b). For the reading of this place-name see D.O. Edzard, RGTC 1, 183; K. Volk, N.A.B.U. 1997/60.

URUxA^{ki} (= **uru'a**?): A city conquered by Eannatum (16 ii 6). For a possible reading *urua see RGTC 1, 181; but also note MSL 14, 432, C 6'-7'.

zimbir^{ki} (*sippa/ir*) [(28:17]: The city of the sun-god where Hammurapi built a canal.

For particulars about each place see the appropriate entry in RGTC 1 and 2.

SACRED BUILDINGS

a-ḫuš (21 i 20): Syllabic writing of é-ḫuš, "Fearsome House". Ningirsu's sanctuary built by Enmetena (*Gazetteer, n. 491*).

abzu: It is normally written ZU.AB, as in 37:24; but in 36:20 it is written ab-zu. It is Enki's underwater dwelling. The word refers to a cultic structure. In 41 i 4 it means Enki's sanctuary at Pasirra (*Gazetteer, n. 31*).

an-ta-sur-ra (18 ii 1; 21 ii 18): "(House) which Twinkles from Heaven". Ningirsu's sanctuary, dating to at least the time of Urnanše (*Gazetteer, n. 83*).

ba-gára (in our texts it appears only in the personal name ur-ba-gára [38 iv 47]): Ningirsu's sanctuary in Lagaš (*Gazetteer, n. 96*).

bur-sag̃ (18 iv 2): "Foremost Jar". A kind of building (part of a temple(?), cf. PSD B 187 2.1). There was more than one bur-sag̃ since various gods had one (FAOS 5/2 124f. ad 'Entemena' 33, note 3). Its epithet is é-sá-du_{11}-an-na(-ta$^{!}$)-IL_2-a-ni "His House from which Regular Offerings are delivered to him (Ningirsu)" (*Gazetteer, n. 129*).

é-ad-da (18 iii 8; 21 i 2, iv 3, vi 6): "House of the Father". The sanctuary of Enlil, Ningirsu's father. Its exact location is unknown (*Gazetteer, n. 40*).

é-an-na (23 i 5, iv 3): "House of Heaven", Inanna's temple in G̃irsu. It probably owed its name to the é-an-na in Uruk, Inanna's most important cult center (*Gazetter n.* 77).

é-^{d}anzu^{mušen}-bábbar (8:8): "House, White Anzu". The name of this temple is attested only on brick inscriptions found at G̃irsu, Tell I (see AnOr 30, 121; 123, a-ga-erena).

é-^{d}ba-U_2 (18 iii 5): "Temple of Ba'U", built by IriKAgina (see AWL, 198f. ad 46 III 2).

é-bábbar (17:2): "White House". This is not Utu's famous temple in Zimbir/*Sippar*, but a temple in the state of Lagaš. According to G.J. Selz, FAOS 15/1, 194, it was dedicated to Ningirsu (*Gazetteer, n. 99*).

é-bàppir (18 ii 6; 19:14): "House of Beer-Bread"; the brewery, part of the é-ninnu where beer seems to have been brewed. Its epithet was g̃eštin$^{!}$ sìla-gal-[gal] kur-ta de_6-a "(to which) Grape Juice Has Been Brought in 'Big' Liter-Vessels from the Mountain Regions".

é-engur-ra (21 ii 7): "House of the Abyss". Nanše's temple located at Sulum near Lagaš, built by Enmetena (*Gazetteer, n. 250*).

é-^{d}ĝá-tùm-du$_{10}$(-g) [21 ii 22]: "Ĝatumdu's temple", located in Iriku in Ĝirsu (*Gazetteer, n. 1314*).

é-gal-ti-ra-áš (18 i 8): "Palace of Tiraš". Ninĝirsu's sanctuary dating to at least the time of Urnanše (*Gazetteer, n. 1097*).

é-gal-uru$_{x}$(URUxKAR$_{2}$)^{ki}(-b) [20:22; 21 ii 4]: "Palace of Uru(b)". Temple of Lugal-uru(b), located at Uru(b)" (*Gazetteer, n. 1351*).

é-ĝéštu-šu-du$_{7}$ (29:25): "House that Perfects Understanding". Enki's temple in Ur (*Gazetteer, n. 364*).

é-ĝidru (10 rev. 3; 24 ii 11): "House of the Sceptre", a seven-cornered house (é-ub-imin). Part of the é-ninnu (*Gazetteer, n. 393*).

é-^{ĝiš}gígir (13:6; 18 ii 3): "Chariot House". Part of the é-ninnu where Ninĝirsu's chariot was kept (see AnOr 30 126, 15). Its epithet was é me-li$_{9}$-bi kur-kur-ra dul$_{5}$ (18 ii 4) "House whose Splendor Covers the Mountains" (*Gazetteer, n. 766*).

é-iri-kù-ga (10 rev. 5; 26 iii 7): "House of the Pure City". Temple of Ba'U in the sacred quarter of Ĝirsu (*Gazetteer, n. 1198*).

é-^{d}lugal-uru$_{x}$(URUxKAR$_{2}$)^{ki}(-b) [20:32]: "Temple of Lugaluru(b)", located in Uru(b) (*Gazetteer, n. 1351*).

é-maḫ (22 ii 5): "Sublime House". While this is the name of Ninḫursaĝ's temple in Ĝirsu, it is uncertain whether our passage refers to the temple by name, or whether the phrase simply means "sublime house" (*Gazetteer, n. 716*).

é-me-ḫuš-gal-an-ki (18 iii 3) "House of the Great Furious Me's of Heaven and Earth/Underworld". Igalim's temple in Ĝirsu (*Gazetteer, n. 755*).

é-mùš (in the PN ur-é-mùš, 33 i 3; 34 vi 3): "House, Foundation (of the Land)". Dumuzi's temple in Badtibira (*Gazetteer, n. 829*).

é-ninnu (5:6; 10 rev. 1; 22 r. sh. 4; 23 ii 8; 24 v 9; PN ur-é-ninnu 38:7) also called é-ninnu-^{d}anzu^{mušen}-bábbar (7 ii 2; 24 ii 7; 25 i 9): "House-Fifty" and "House-Fifty, White Anzu". The most important sacred building in the state of Lagaš, it was Ninĝirsu's temple-complex in Ĝirsu (cf. AnOr 30, 116-143). Its name shows that it incarnated the fifty *me*. This is clear from Gudea, cylinder A x 6. It dated to the time of Urnanše (12 ii 1: èš-g̃ír-sú) but was substantially rebuilt by Gudea (*Gazetteer, n. 897*).

é-sá-du$_{11}$-an-na-ta$^{!}$-IL$_{2}$-a-ni (18 iv 3): "His House from which Regular Offerings are Delivered to him (Ning̃irsu)". Epithet of the bur-sag̃.

é-šu-sè-ga (29:29): "Cella", "Temple Chamber"; Part of Enki's temple é-g̃éštu-šu-du$_7$ in Ur.

é-TAR-sír-sír (26 ii 1; iii 3): Temple of Ba'U. Originally it was at Lagaš but was transferred by Gudea to G̃irsu (*Gazetteer, n. 1086*).

èš-DUG.RU (21 i 18): "Sanctuary (in?) DUG.RU" that belonged to Ning̃irsu (*Gazetteer, n. 1375*).

gi-gù-na (*gigunû*): A building ('reed chamber') constructed on a terrace for Ning̃irsu [11:4 (èš-gi gi-gù-na)] (*Gazetteer, n.* 1376); for Ninḫursag̃ in Tirku(-g) [21 ii 14]; for Nanše [21 iii 2] (*Gazetteer, n. 1362*).

gi-gunu$_4$ (24 ii 9): An alternate spelling of gi-gù-na. Here it designates the edifice located in the é-ninnu.

ib (*tubuqtu*; 44 i 7): "Temple Niche(?)", see FAOS 6, 167 s.v.

ib-gal (37:20, in PN lú-ib-gal): "Big Niche(?)". Inanna's temple complex in the city of Lagaš (*Gazetteer, n. 505*).

ki-tuš-akkil-lé (18 ii 9): "Abode of Lamentation". Šulšagana's shrine at G̃irsu (in the é-ninnu? - *Gazetteer, n. 618*).

šà-pà-da (21 ii 20): "(House) Called in the Heart", i.e. "Chosen House" Nanše's temple in the city of Lagaš (*Gazetteer, n. 1022*).

For *further information* about the buildings mentioned above see A.R. George, House Most High. The Temples of Ancient Mesopotamia. Mesopotamian Civilizations 5 (Winona Lake 1993). '*Gazetteer*' in the Glossary refers to p. 63-161 of this book.

YEAR DATES

YEAR-DATES OF PRE-SARGONIC ADMINISTRATIVE TEXTS

Text 33 = (Lugalanda) 6

Text 34 = (Lugalanda) 3

Text 40 = (IriKAgina) 2

Text 41 = (Lugalanda) 2

Text 42 = (IriKAgina) 2

Text 43 = (Lugalanda) 6

Text 44 = (IriKAgina) undated

For the dating system in these texts see no. 257 in the Sign List.

YEAR NAMES

For the year names in the Ur III administrative texts, see the references in M. Sigrist and T. Gomi, The Comprehensive Catalogue of Published Ur III Tablets (Bethesda [MD] 1991). The variant writings of the individual year names are listed in N. Schneider, Die Zeitbestimmungen der Wirtschaftsurkunden von Ur III (Rome 1936), 30ff. ('4. Gimilsin' [= *Šusîn*]).

Text 31 = *Šusîn* 8 (see M. Sigrist/T. Gomi, Catalogue, 327)

Text 32 = *Šusîn* 6 (see M. Sigrist/T. Gomi, Catalogue, 327)

Text 36 = *Šusîn* 3a (see M. Sigrist/T. Gomi, Catalogue, 327)

Text 37 = *Šusîn* 2 (see M. Sigrist/T. Gomi, Catalogue, 326)

Text 38 = *Šusîn* 4a (M. Sigrist/T. Gomi, Catalogue, 327)

FESTIVALS

Text 41: ezem-amar-a-a-si-ge$_4$-da (see M.E. Cohen, Cultic Calendars, 58-60; G.J. Selz, UGASL, 258f. sub 8; J. Bauer, AfO 36/37 [1989/90] 88f.)

Text 42: ezem-^{d}ba-U$_2$ (see M.E. Cohen, Cultic Calendars, 53-54; G.J. Selz, UGASL, 70 sub 149, 72 sub 152)

Text 43: ezem-še-gu$_7$-^{d}nanše (see M.E. Cohen, Cultic Calendars, 44-46)

Text 44: ezem-an-ta-sur-ra (see M.E. Cohen, Cultic Calendars, 57; G.J. Selz, UGASL, 240 sub 100; 242f. sub 110)

Finito di stampare nel mese di aprile 1999
presso la tipografia “Giovanni Olivieri”
00187 Roma - Via dell’Archetto, 10,11,12